What Our Clients Say About Us

I endorse the New School Selling training as the most effective selling system I have ever been taught. It is impossible to argue with the irrefutable logic of results.

**DEVIN B. WARNER, FORMER VP MEMBERSHIP SERVICES,
PENSACOLA, FL CHAMBER OF COMMERCE**

Many of the sales and negotiations suggestions have already been implemented at the Chamber and I find that we are dealing with members and prospective members in a more professional and caring manner.

**KAREN TOMASOVIC, FORMER EXECUTIVE DIRECTOR
GULF BREEZE, FL CHAMBER OF COMMERCE**

The coaching suggestions you initially made resulted in an INCREASE of $16,000 in first year life insurance commissions the first thirty days we worked together.

**FLETCHER MCKINNEY, ADVANTAGE INSURANCE AGENCY, INC.
TAMPA, FL**

My closing rate has changed from about 15% to approximately 70% in one year and this year will be my most profitable year in four years.

**CRAIG BREITSPRECHER, LACROSSE SIGN COMPANY
LACROSSE, WISCONSIN**

How do you take a young woman with NO sales experience and give her the training and confidence to sell $50,000 cases to prospects? Oh, and how do you do that without sending her to expensive, out of town seminars and incur both travel costs and downtime? And how do you get her long time support? Easy. You enroll her in a TeleClass course with Steve Clark, that's how ... Simple, easy and effective training for novice to experienced sales personnel.

**DR. CURTIS WESTERSUND, COSMETIC RESTORATION DENTIST
CALGARY, ALBERTA, CANADA**

Working with Steve Clark over the last several years has made a real difference in our sales results. Utilizing the New School Sales Management process we have become more focused on those sales behaviors that make a difference. Thank you Steve.

RANDOLPH M. POPLE, PRESIDENT, CAPITAL CITY TRUST COMPANY,
TALLAHASSEE, FL

In August, my team set a State Farm record for all of North Florida agents, and through September 10th, we are 45% ahead of last month. My investment in sales training for my staff is paying off handsomely.

STEVE FIFER, CLU, STATE FARM
PENSACOLA, FL

Our sales are up 289% year to date. We have already exceeded last year's first quarter by over 200%. Things are booming over here.

PATRICK ROONEY, CPA, PRESIDENT, NUOVO TECHNOLOGIES, INC.
NAVARRE, FL

Steve is a valuable resource for our company. His insight, training and coaching have helped us grow and improve our company's sales revenues and profits. I highly recommend his service to anyone who is committed to growing their company.

BART WELLS, PRESIDENT, SPERRY AND ASSOCIATES, INC., (COMMERCIAL CONTRACTORS)
TALLAHASSEE, FL

Each week I look forward to class. It's kind of like going to church in that I get recharged each week. Now that I have been in the program for four months, the light bulbs are flashing almost weekly as I come to understand and utilize each new concept.

RICK REYNOLDS, CEO, VENUE, (MESSAGE ON HOLD COMPANY)
NAVARRE, FL

Thank you for the "education" you have provided over the last two years. The New School system of selling has proved to be the best investment I have ever made in myself and my business.

DAVE KELEHER, AMSTAFF HUMAN RESOURCES
PENSACOLA, FL

We have seen measurable results using the systems taught in Steve's training. By implementing these techniques, we have been able to consistently close more than 70% of our proposals.

JIM NITTERAUER, PRESIDENT, CREATIVE DATA CONCEPTS LIMITED, INC.
PENSACOLA, FL

The things I have learned since joining your training have been extremely rewarding and quite frankly, more than I had anticipated. My recurring annual sales have increased by more than $40,000. In doing so, I have made far fewer presentations and spent far less time on these sales.

RICH MOORE, PRESIDENT, ENVIRONMENTAL BIOTECH
PENSACOLA, FL

I am closing 92% of all my proposals. The system truly works! I've been blessed with you as a trainer and as a mentor. I know that I am fortunate to have discovered you and your services.

CHRIS DEHLIC, SALES MANAGER, CREATIVE DATA CONCEPTS LIMITED, INC.
PENSACOLA, FL

I have been involved in this program since last year. Here is what happened: my sales in a month are equal to what I used to make in an entire year! It is amazing to me. I have even been successful using the system over the phone since 98% of my business is out of town and I never have a face-to-face appointment.

PHYLLIS DAVIS-MINIK, PRESIDENT, ADVANCED EDI & BARCODING CORP.
PENSACOLA, FL

Your training has resulted in a dramatic increase in my sales. Since I began your training sales this year are 271% greater than sales for the same time last year. This increase is due to both the techniques and continuous reinforcement that you offer.

PAUL WHITE, PAUL WHITE PHOTOGRAPHY,
PENSACOLA, FL

I have been in sales for over 8 years and have attended dozens of sales seminars. The most informative seminar that I have ever attended was "New School Selling" presented by Steve Clark. The Jump Start Sales Skills Training course that Steve offered was awesome. His one suggestion of receiving 100 yes or no's through cold calling landed me 56 appointments in two short weeks of cold calling!

TAMMY TIBBENS, SENIOR ACCOUNT EXECUTIVE, CLEAR CHANNEL
HARRISBURG, PA

Last month Flanagan Instruments, Inc.'s Surgical Specialties division broke a single month sales record, which had stood for four years. While that milestone was exciting, it is also important to note that in the last eight months the division has had four of the top seven selling months, in dollar volume, in the sixteen-year history of the division. Of course, many factors went into these record setting sales, but, in my opinion, the training our sales force began receiving from you in October 2001 was a major contributor to the success.

ROBERT BYRNE, VICE PRESIDENT, FLANAGAN INSTRUMENTS
MANDEVILLE, LA

As a result of the Steve's training in sales management we reorganized our sales department actually reducing the budget for the department. We sent the sales staff to a live New School Selling course and did a follow up course via phone/web. In the following twelve months, our ad agency landed double the number of new accounts we had achieved in any other previous twelve month period. The training helped us in a number of areas, giving us some tracks to run on for prospecting and teaching us how to uncover the real needs of prospects and existing clients.

CHRIS BUSCH, PRESIDENT, BIZDREAMS, LLC
TULSA, OK

We have used Steve's training materials both for sales managers training as well as sale people training at our annual sales conference. His training materials are easy to implement, and practical for managers and sellers. Sales Managers and sales people can take what they learn from Steve's to the streets with immediate results. His interview questions and hiring tools are also excellent for sales managers.

TED WALDBILLIG, DIRECTOR OF SALES, MID-WEST FAMILY BROADCASTING
MADISON, WISCONSIN

Clark-McKibben Safety Products and myself were introduced to Steve Clark and New School Selling, Inc. through a teleconference in March of 2007. As a small company, nine full time employees, I wear many hats and therefore am pulled in many directions. At the time I met Steve I was attempting to set new goals for our company and replace a salesperson.

Steve offered guidance through both the monthly TeleClass training sessions and our one-on-one coaching calls. We developed a plan not only for the recruiting process but also for the first ninety days for our new salesperson. We received a bag full of applicants and by using developed criteria and TriMetrix testing we narrowed down the list to two. Using the New School interview techniques we hired our new salesperson. He has been with C-M one month. Last week was his first week he made sales calls on his own. He had no experience in our field, however, in his first week he has brought seven new business opportunities. One key moment for me since I began working with Steve was when he asked me how much time we would spend with a $300,000 customer. Since our salespeople generate that much and more maybe we should spend that much time and money on growing and developing our sales staff.

JACK MCKIBBEN PRESIDENT / CEO, CLARK-MCKIBBEN SAFETY PRODUCTS, INC.
ERIE, PA

I'm in radio advertising sales and marketing. Your training was MORE than I expected. I found your training to be "an awakening" in certain areas. For example...when it came to talking about MONEY with clients and prospects...I would often be hesitant or tip-toe around the subject. But from your training, I'm now able to talk about it freely with prospects. What does that do for me? It's saved me a ton of time! And I always need more of that! It saved me time by finding out early in a conversation whether or not somebody could afford my product and services. Why waste time with someone that doesn't have the money? Of course I don't sell on price…but I'm not afraid to tell them my price (even though it's a little higher than most) because it's more than worth it. Another great thing I utilize from your training is the use of an agenda. When I have meetings with prospects…I give them an agenda of what we will cover in a meeting. That way…I am more focused…rather than shooting from the hip. AND the prospect knows that I mean business…and they come to their OWN conclusion that I don't want to waste THEIR time. What has it done for my sales? Well, within a year my sales increased of 20%.

DUANE CHRISTENSEN, RADIO MARKETING GUY, RESULTS RADIO, CUMULUS MEDIA SIOUX FALLS

My results from working with you have been nothing short of amazing. By "letting go" of my ways and adopting the approaches you teach I have realized a huge increase in my sales. Comparing my numbers from all of 2006 to what I've accomplished through the end of October 2007 shows almost a 100% increase!

Most importantly have been the life-changing aspects of your training. I can tell you that my life is better because my attitude has greatly improved; I have learned better ways to approach life's daily challenges. Your training and coaching have helped me to grow, not only as a consultant, but also as a person.

RICK STEVENS SHALIMAR, FL

Your seminar was the first time I ever felt compelled to actually BUY anything. I was with you 100% of the day….it all made so much sense. I've been listening to your entire CD set……got my goals and affirmations written on index cards.

I am seeing significant changes in not only the way I view myself, but clients and prospects as well. Thanks so much for the awakening.

CURTIS SMITH, ACCOUNT EXECUTIVE, CLEAR CHANNEL RADIO
HARRISBURG, PA

Since we have begun New School Selling, changes both personally and within the organization have been unbelievable. As a result of our training our organization no longer chases business. We have eliminated a lot of wasted time by changing our beliefs and making customers qualify to do business with our company. By doing this we actually turn down people who are just shopping. We now develop business (and relationships) rather than chase business. My closing rate has changed from about 15% to approximately 70% in one year and this year will be my profitable year in four years.

CRAIG BREITSPRECHER, LACROSSE SIGN COMPANY
LACROSSE, WISCONSIN

It's been ten years since we teamed up with Steve Clark. The rewards have been phenomenal. Steve's guidance and enthusiasm, and my hard work have resulted in an income and life style far beyond my wildest expectations. Steve's teaching has indeed changed my life!

TED WOODARD, LACROSSE SIGN CO.
LACROSSE, WISCONSIN

We have had the pleasure of working with Steve Clark as our organization's sales trainer and personal sales coach for the last three years. Steve's training and coaching has dramatically increased the sales production and motivation of both our experienced and new producers.

BILL GUNTER, FORMER INSURANCE COMMISSIONER OF FLORIDA,
CHAIRMAN, ROGERS, GUNTER, VAUGHN INSURANCE, INC.
TALLAHASSEE, FL

Super Achievers have an Abundant Mentality. Steve's ability to help our producers develop and maintain this attitude is one of the reasons that he continues to be one of the most influential outside consultants that we use at First Protective.

ANDY MARTIN, CLU, CHFC, PRESIDENT, FIRST PROTECTIVE
BIRMINGHAM, AL

With in hours of listening to Steve I had already changed some of my fundamentals beliefs. Throughout the course Steve showed me how I can change my habits to reflect these new beliefs and in turn change the course of my life. Do not be fooled it is not easy, it takes time and commitment but anything worth doing always does. I have been following Steve's advice since going to the course and I have seen the benefits.

JASON L. FITTLER, CPA (FPS), B.COM, DFP
TOWNSVILLE, QUEENSLAND AUSTRALIA

Steve struck several nerves with me. The point that really resonated with me was the strategy to manage frustrations, associated with rejection. I have always thought that I was self aware, that I knew my limits. My four years in the Marine Corps made me think that I was mentally tough. I have come to the conclusion that it doesn't matter how tough you are. If you don't have a strategy for deflecting rejection, at some point it will probably wear you down.

MIKE GOFF CLEAR CHANNEL
LIMA, OH

All reports are that your breakout session was well received. I received a number of postitive comments throughout the rest of the Convention. Our members noted your solid, down-to-earth content, as well as, your excellent presentation skills. You presented a great deal of information that agents in Florida need to know.

CINDY MOLNAR, CMP, MEETING PLANNER
FLORIDA ASSOCIATION OF INSURANCE AGENTS

When I started with your coaching I was deeply entrenched in burnout and couldn't figure a way out. Using you as a coach has not only increased our sales but we are having fun selling again and my staff is fired up with all the new revenues.

DUKE MILLS, PRESIDENT
WORKCOMP SOLUTIONS, INC., LAKELAND, FL

Steve, with your help and coaching, I was able to qualify for membership in the MDRT Top of the Table for the first time in my twenty-four years in the Life Insurance business. In addition to having a great business year, I was also able to take more time off to spend with my family and feel more comfortable doing so.

JOHN CURRY, CLU, CHFC, NORTH FLORIDA FINANCIAL
TALLAHASSEE, FL

Last year was a productive one for me. Utilizing your ideas and weekly coaching, I was our firm's "top gun". I produced higher commissions than any of my prior twenty years in this business. The discussions and roll play we had prior to one appointment helped me place one life case that paid me over $40,000 in commissions. The time I used to spend chasing prospects and hoping for results is now better utilized. I feel more confident and energized than I have for years.

JOHN HOWARD, CLU, CHFC, CFP, ROGERS, GUNTER,VAUGHN INSURANCE, INC.
TALLAHASSEE, TALLAHASSEE, FL

As my persoal Sales Coach, your analysis of my selling process has been eye opening. The coaching suggestions you initially made resulted in an INCREASE of $16,000 in first year life insurance commissions the first 30 days we worked together. Not only have I increased my income but I have done so by working fewer hours than ever before.

FLETCHER MCKINNEY, OWNER, ADVANTAGE INSURANCE AGENCY, INC.
LAKELAND, FL

As a Certified Financial Planner, I was frustrated with my sales process which wasted a lot of time and was ineffective. Since working with Steve Clark and learning a new more effective sales process, I have learned how to stay in control of the sales process and eliminate wasted time with prospects that are not committed to improving their financial future. My performance has increased substantially and I am now enjoying my career more than ever.

GARY PARSONS, CFP, ROGERS, ATKINS, GUNTER AND ASSOCIATES
TALLAHASSEE, FL

I have been in the Financial Services Business for nearly fifteen years. The approach offered by your company is the first truly new and worthwhile approach I have seen in this period of time. Your coaching has provided me with new tools to be more effective in the financial services profession.

J. SCOTT FENSTERMAKER, BENEFITS CONSULTANT, LANDRUM-YAGER FINANCIAL SERVICES
TALLAHASSEE, FL

Steve is a valuable resource for our company. His insight, training, and coaching have helped us grow and improve our company's sales revenues and profits. I highly recommend his service to anyone who is committed to growing their company.

BART WELLS, PRESIDENT, SPERRY & ASSOCIATES, INC.
TALLAHASSEE, FL

For this year our sales are 289% ahead of YTD last year. We have already exceeded last year's first quarter by over 200%. Things are booming over here.

PATRICK ROONE, CPA, PRESIDENT, NUOVO TECHNOLOGIES, INC.
PENSACOLA, FL

We have seen measurable results using the Sales Warrior techniques. By implementing these techniques we have been able to consistently close more than 70% of our proposals!

JIM NITTERAUER, PRESIDENT, CREATIVE DATA CONCEPTS
PENSACOLA, FL

Since participating in your training, my annual recurring sales have increased by over $40,000 annually. I have done this by giving fewer presentations and *spending far less time than I used to. I am now being paid for consulting that I used to do for free. And on top of this our very satisfied customers are helping us grow by referring others.*

RICH MOORE, PRESIDENT, ENVIRONMENTAL BIOTECH
PENSACOLA, FL

In August you helped us pinpoint our exact goals, outlining the exact dollar amount we needed in increased sales to take our business to the next level. Since we began using your services, every quarter's billing has been larger and more profitable than the previous quarter. As of May's issue, we've reached the billing goals you helped us outline last year. I'm looking forward to the results of learning and mastering even more in the upcoming months.

DAVID BANKS, OWNER, DASH PUBLISHING, INC.
PENSACOLA, FL

As a Sales Director for an Insurance Marketing Firm, I needed weekly account-ability and sales training. Steve was able to help me sharpen my interviewing skills and ask the right questions to get financial service professionals to commit to doing business with First Protective. Without Steve, I may have wasted a tremen-dous amount of time, asking the wrong questions of the wrong people.

Today I am a top performing sales director and have maintained consistent per-formance each year by doing the things I learned from Steve.

JAY STUBBS, CLU FIRST PROTECTIVE
MOBILE, AL

In the short time you have been with us, not only have I increased my sales revenue, but I am much more confident I will attain my professional as well as personal goals in 2009! Your training has not only helped me become a better listener, but more importantly sharpened my line of "asking questions" which has helped me work more efficiently and position myself much more professional than other salespeople in my industry. From setting the agenda, to quickly disqualify-ing prospects who are not worth pursuing, I have found I now have more time to help people who really have the means, desire and need for professional marketing guidance.

RUBEN LEVISMAN, LINCOLN FINANCIAL MEDIA
MIAMI, FL

I used your discovery questionnaire before meeting with a prospect. It (along with the agenda and asking tough questions) landed me a client with about $600k to rollover. I'll make about $6k per year of that account, plus the life insurance and other stuff he needs.

MARK EVERS
AUSTIN, TX

Steve Clark's dynamic program improves your bottom line results by starting where it matters most – on the inside, where your belief systems and attitude strongly influence outcomes. Then he takes you to the real world – face to face - where results depend on your effectiveness in front of others. He teaches you that results are not about your presentation; not about your price; not about your product. As a former sales trainer for a world-wide sales organization, I had a number of Ah-Ha experiences working with Steve. His unique techniques helped me take my business to even higher levels. His secrets will help you generate extraordinary sales and life results in short order.

LARRY PARMAN, ATTORNEY
OVERLAND PARK, KS

Thank-you very much for today's class, it was fantastic and I jotted down "Copious" amounts of notes. Dave and I always say that it's such a confidence booster for the rest of the week and today you exceeded my expectations big time.

RYAN KOVARIK, ACCOUNT REPRESENTATIVE, CJCS-AM/CHGK-FM
STRATFORD, ONTARIO

Steve Clark and New Schooling Selling have greatly influenced my view of sales prospecting and recruiting sales professionals. His "cut to the chase" approach has instilled a sense of urgency with my sales staff and provided me with a sense of accountability.

Perhaps the greatest benefit has been adopting Steve's approach to recruiting and qualifying sales professionals. Using a reliable survey system and coaching from Steve, I quickly separate hunters from gatherers. I have set realistic expectations of my sales staff and I have increased confidence in my assessment of new hires ability to sell.

JOHN SCHOLL, CEO, BIG INK
SEATTLE, WA

I just wanted to say thanks for your help last week. I did what you suggested... the 100% guarantee... and I just got a call from the vendor... they are in. So we have our first sponsor @ $5000.

JANE DUEEASE, GROWING YOUNG EXPO
AUSTIN, TX

I have been in sales for years, but until I met Steve, I never really knew how to sell effectively. Through one-on-one coaching, Steve has given me the tools to overcome my selling mistakes and drive more opportunities into my pipeline. Along the way, he's taught me to think more strategically, communicate better and balance my time.

CARYN BROWN, SECURITY SOFTWARE CHANNEL SALES
NORTH CAROLINA

Do you possess a flagging sales process? Enter Steve Clark and New School Selling. Renewed optimism leads to increased prospects, increased transference of confidence and ultimately increased sales. I know because I've been such a possessor, then a student and now Manager of a successful sales force. New School Selling makes me look good. No BS (bad selling), just honesty.

STEVE RAE, PRESIDENT/GENERAL MANAGER, RAEDIO INC.
STRATFORD, CANADA

I have had some good years selling but the last few have been a struggle to meet monthly goals. New School Selling was the difference between continuing to struggle or exceeding monthly budgets by as much as 23% in the course of a few short months. The processes and information we discuss each week are relevant and have given me more confidence then what I ever had before. It's exciting to think that I'm still very new in this training but have already seen such powerful change in my ability to do my job better for myself, company and clients. great success."

CHRIS PEARSON, ASSISTANT SALES MANAGER, CKBW FM 93.1 94.5
BRIDGEWATER, NS, CANADA

Throw everything you think you know about sales out the window. Let Steve Clark introduce you or your sales staff to new-school selling. I would highly recommend the new school selling system and techniques that Steve teaches. If you are in sales and want to leave your competition in the dust Steve is your man to educate and motivate your sales team. Steve's system will teach you to use your time more efficiently and increase your sales.

DAVE ELLIOTT, RADIO ACCOUNT REPRESENTATIVE
STRATFORD, ONTARIO, CANADA

The New School Selling Approach to doing a good uncovery was instrumental in maintaining a $1,000,000 account, The Tuscon Auto Mall for the Tuscon Citizen Newspaper.

KELLY WARE BARNES
LAS VEGAS, NV

Profitable Persuasion

Put the Hay Down Where the Goats Can Get it.

Profitable Persuasion

Put the Hay Down Where the Goats Can Get it.

Proven Strategies for Sales and Management Success

Steve Clark

Published by Advantage, Charleston, South Carolina.
Member of Advantage Media Group.

ADVANTAGE is a registered trademark and the Advantage colophon is a trademark of Advantage Media Group, Inc.

Printed in the United States of America.

ISBN: 978-1-59932-087-8
LCCN: 2008943880

Most Advantage Media Group titles are available at special quantity discounts for bulk purchases for sales promotions, premiums, fundraising, and educational use. Special versions or book excerpts can also be created to fit specific needs.

For more information, please write: Special Markets, Advantage Media Group, P.O. Box 272, Charleston, SC 29402 or call 1.866.775.1696.

Visit us online at **advantagefamily**.com

This book is dedicated to:

My loving wife Charleen who has always believed in me even when I didn't believe in myself.

CONTENTS

WHO IS STEVE CLARK AND WHY SHOULD YOU LISTEN TO HIM

Steve is a scrapper and an over comer. Early in his sales career he struggled financially, was dead broke, had his water cut off for lack of payment and was almost bankrupt. He has been sued by a competitor who tried to put him out of business. But he has always "reloaded and fired again" no matter the struggle or no matter the circumstance. Perhaps his great asset is that he doesn't know the word quit.

What Is Steve's Background

Steve grew up in a modest military family where his father was an Army sergeant and his mother was a waitress. From the 7th grade through high school graduation his entire four person family lived in a 72 foot long by 12 foot wide house trailer.

He certainly has never been fed with a silver spoon.

Everything he has achieved – and he has achieved a lot - has come because he is not a quitter and has persisted and chased his dreams while staring adversity in the face.

Steve's introduction to selling came at age 11 when he began selling flower seeds and greeting cards door to door for *Boys Life* magazine. As a young door to door salesman he experienced a lot of rejection and failure but that didn't deter him from winning the prizes and awards that were advertised in the magazine. At thirteen he began selling and delivering 73 daily newspapers on his bicycle. In addition to selling and delivering, each week he had to go by his customers house and collect either the weekly or monthly fee. More experience collecting and soliciting door to door. In high school he sold more candy and raised more money for the prom than any of his other 248 junior classmates.

After high school, Steve attended college at the University of South Carolina where he obtained a Bachelor's and Master's degree in education. After graduating he worked for 5 years in public health for the state of South Carolina. This was a short lived career that set the stage for his entry into the world of professional selling in 1980.

What Real Sales Experience Does He Have

Since 1980, he has sold pest control services, pots and pans, security systems, vitamins, laundry detergent, life and health insurance, annuities, mutual funds, stocks and bonds and raised over $1,000,000 for schools in Northwest Florida.

Steve is a self taught sales person who has read hundreds of sales, management, and psychology books, listened to thousands of hours of audio recordings, attended scores and scores of sales seminars and most importantly made over 10,000 face to face or telephone prospecting calls.

He is the ultimate Sales Warrior.

The Big Break Through

In 1996, Steve was making $53,000 per year as a salesperson and he had over $40,000 of credit card debt. Taking out a second mortgage on his house and borrowing $10,000 from his Mother, he set out into the world of sales and marketing consulting with zero clients, zero income, a wife and two daughters aged 10 and 13.

Sure it was a crazy gamble and one that very, very few people would have the guts to do. But Steve believed in himself and knew that he had the desire and work ethic to do whatever it would take to achieve his dream of financial freedom and total control of his life and his destiny.

It was an outrageous leap of faith and a gutsy decision that has paid HUGE dividends!

What Were The Results

In his first 12 months in business Steve increased his yearly income to over $110,000. That was more than double what he had previously made in any of his 16 years in sales. Using strategies, tactics and techniques that he was developing and implementing , the following year he doubled his income again to over $220,000…..and in his 3rd year in business he increased his income again to over $353,000. That's a 700% increase in income in 3 years.

Fast Forward To Today

Today, as CEO of **New School Selling,** he heads an international business development and marketing firm that consults and coaches thousands of sales executives and business owners annually in Australia, Canada and the US. He routinely gets paid $9400.00 daily to consult and deliver training for his clients. In 2007, his consulting fees were in excess of $500,000.00.

He is the author of the audio books:

- Cultivating an Abundant Mentality

- Live Down Under

- Golden Keys to More Effective Sales Management

- Prospecting to Fill the Pipeline

- Tools and Tactics For Profitable Persuasion

He is a guest columnist of Radio Ink magazine and is a frequent national and international speaker.

In addition to his duties as CEO, he is a US Coast Guard Captain and runs a fishing charter business out of Navarre, Florida where many nights you'll find him offshore hauling in Yellow Fin Tuna.

Today he earns more in a month than he used to earn in a year and the thing he loves to do more than anything else in this world is to teach other sales executives how to do the same.

Why Should Any Of This Matter To You

That's a fair question. If you have the desire to excel in the sales profession Steve can help you double or triple your income and obtain a lifestyle you have never imagined. He has learned through the "school of hard knocks" and can help you avoid the pitfalls and wasted time that he had to endure to learn the lessons necessary for sales success.

As A New School Student What Can You Expect

When you become a New School student you will be given a tested and <u>proven system that has a twelve year track record of producing tens millions of dollars of revenue for his clients.</u>

Specifically, New School Selling strategies, tactics and techniques will help you:

1. Shortening the sales cycle

2. Save tons of time that is wasted with non qualified buyers

3. Improve closing percentages

4. Eliminate "free consulting"

5. Increase the number of qualified leads and prospects

6. Weeding out non buyers earlier

7. Reduce discounting in competitive situations

8. Improve negotiation strategies

9. Dramatically increasing your income

You will not have to reinvent the wheel. Simply learn the system, put your foot on the accelerator and take off. All of your time and energy will be spent implementing, doing and **<u>making vast sums of money.</u>**

<u>If you are tired of hearing platitudes and worn out motivational crap then his New School Selling process will be like a breath of fresh air.</u>

As a serious student of New School Selling you will become more bold and confident and will develop a backbone of steel. No longer will buyers be able to jerk you around and treat you like some circus animal that is expected to jump through hoops.

Not only will buyers come to respect you more, <u>you will come to respect yourself and the profession of selling more. And, oh yea, your income will skyrocket into the stratosphere.</u>

Warning: New School Selling is not for everyone. It is not for the lazy, unmotivated or those who think the world owes them something. But if you have a "burning desire" to become one of the top sellers in your industry <u>it can be your ticket to financial freedom and a lifestyle that is the envy of most people.</u>

CHAPTER 1: PROSPECTING

....

Understanding the Biggest Problem in Sales

Why Don't Sales People Prospect Enough?

Virtually every business owner or sales manager have I have ever coached or consulted has listed lack of consistent prospecting by their sales organization as one of the most damaging issues facing their company. This pervasive issue has a long term, crippling financial impact on both companies and their sales people.

While few managers would disagree that this is a major problem, most of them have little understanding of why this is a problem or how to solve it.

Why don't salespeople consistently prospect?

Fear of rejection. Most prospecting behaviors produce a different result than the positive response sales people were hoping or expecting to get? This experience is internalized by the salesperson as some kind of personal failure. This internalization by the sales person makes no sense and only occurs because the sales person has confused external validation by the buyer with personal worth.

Solution: *Help your sales person psychologically reframe their expectation of prospecting and instead of being the rejectee teach them to become the rejector.*

Lack of organization and planning. Most sales people, because of their extroverted personalities, do not have natural organizational and self management skills. They tend to "cock and fire" instead of taking time to develop plans, organize, schedule and execute. The result of their scattered approach is that they waste many hours which could be used to prospect for new business.

Solution: *Teach and require all of your sales people to submit written plans and schedules of their activities each week.*

Not held accountable by management. Most sales mangers have not developed an effective process that holds their sales people accountable to do the necessary prospecting behaviors. They don't know how or are too busy or disinterested to provide the proper coaching and supervision needed by their sales people.

Solution: *Implement a sales management process that teaches and requires sales managers to plan and schedule one on one coaching each week with each sales person.*

Lack of knowledge or lack of skill. Most companies don't offer proper training or coaching on the importance of prospecting, how to develop a prospecting plan, improving personal effectiveness, creative visioning, developing a template of ideal clients, etc.

Solution: *Develop a culture and philosophy of continuous, never ending improvement and invest the time and money to make that a reality.*

And the biggest one of all is the **absence of clearly defined, personally compelling goals.**

All the other things pale in comparison to this one.

The person who has a passionate goal will not be side tracked by rejection, will not need to be held accountable and will succeed in spite of a lack of organizational skills or knowledge. While all of these things will facilitate success they are not requirements for success.

A sales person who is passionate, focused and committed will go out and beat on enough doors until they make it happen. More than anything else when you see call reluctance on a sales person's part it's because they're not passionate about going to the next level or achieving the next goal. They have somehow gotten comfortable with the results that their current behavior is producing for them. And as long as they're satisfied with the results of their current prospecting activities and can live off of the income that's generated from those activities they won't increase their prospecting behaviors.

Solution: *Spend time helping your sales people answer this question.*

Do you have a clearly defined, specific goal that requires you to make more money than you are currently making? Are you absolutely pas-

sionate about it? Are you committed enough to do whatever it takes to achieve that goal as long as it's legal, moral and honest? How can I help you achieve that goal?

Until they can answer WHY the how is unimportant.

....

THE IMPORTANCE OF PROSPECTING

Getting salespeople in front of qualified prospects is typically the number one issue of companies. The ability of the sales force to keep the pipeline full is key to success.

Without an effective prospecting system in place, the sales pipeline is weak which creates pressure to be more aggressive in selling to poorly qualified prospects. This leads to poor sales, deteriorating margins, frustrated salespeople and concerned management.

PROPER PROSPECTING MENTALITY

Prospecting can be equated to ***panning for gold.*** During the Gold Rush days in California, prospectors set up camp by a stream and patiently sifted through pan after pan of gravel and sand in the hopes of finding a gold nugget or two. It was hard, frustrating work, not unlike sales prospecting today. Perhaps the major difference between the gold prospector and the sales prospector is their attitude toward the process. Gold prospectors knew and accepted that they'd have to go through a great deal of gravel and sand to find a nugget. Instead of being frustrated when most of their effort didn't produce results they accepted it as the reality of the job.

Unlike the gold prospector, today's salesperson has an unrealistic expectation of prospecting. Instead of accepting the reality that most of their prospecting efforts will be in vain they believe that their prospecting activity should produce significant results. As a result they become frustrated with each call that doesn't pan out.

To prevent disappointment and frustration salespeople need to change their view of prospecting and remember that ***prospecting is a discarding activity***. The successful salesperson understands that fact and realizes he will need to go through a number of contacts to find the real nugget.

COLD CALLING

Cold calling is only one form of prospecting, but certainly the most stressful. The essence of cold calling is initiating contact with strangers. Research has shown that initiating contact with strangers is the most stressful part of the salesperson's job (didn't mom and dad tell you not to talk to strangers? Well, that old tape may still be playing in your head).

Due to the stress involved, most salespeople have a negative attitude toward cold calling: they don't like to make cold calls and usually have poor cold-calling skills. Some even see it as begging.

Add to the stress of initiating contact with strangers such factors as a high rejection rate (typically far less than 10 percent of cold calls ever result in a sale) and fear of the unknown-What objections will I get? Will he or she be friendly? Will they need what I'm selling? -and you have a recipe for failure.

These are the primary reasons why salespeople leave the profession. Yet those who have overcome these negative attitudes and develop good cold-calling skills are the salespeople who consistently achieve their sales objectives and earn the highest incomes.

CHARACTERISTICS OF A TRADITIONAL COLD CALL

When you think of a cold call, what do you think of? The telemarketer who calls during dinner and won't let you off the phone? The traditional objective is to get someone on the phone, tell them about your product or service and try to convince them that they should buy or at least set an appointment with you.

The underlying belief is that everyone is a prospect and that you're trying to make a sale to everyone. It involves overcoming objections, being doggedly tenacious and not taking NO for an answer. Typically the recipient of the call feels like the salesperson is intruding on his or her time, pushing his agenda down the prospect's throat.

Sounds like this.

> **Andy Gump:** Hi, Mr. Smith, this is Andy Gump from ABC Corporation. How are you this evening?

> **Mr. Smith:** I'm OK. What are you selling?

The prospect knew intuitively that this was a sales call, just based on how Andy started the call.

> **Andy Gump:** I'm not selling anything. I just called to tell you about a great opportunity to . . .
>
> **Mr. Smith:** I'm really not interested.
>
> **Andy:** Are you saying that you wouldn't be interested if I could show you a way to increase your _____ and save you money at the same time?
>
> **Mr. Smith:** Click.

Doesn't this sound like a lot of fun for both parties?

A FRESH APPROACH TO COLD CALLING

A paradigm shift is necessary. ***We must begin to see cold calling as a discarding activity that gets us to a "no" faster while maintaining rapport and integrity.*** The faster you can get through that pan of gravel, the more gravel you can look at and the sooner you'll find some gold.

Not acting like a salesperson is a fundamental change that must be made. The first thing they buy on the telephone is you, and the decision is made within seconds whether they'll talk to you or not. If what you say initially makes you sound like a salesperson, the guard goes up and they'll be trying to get rid of you (remember what a bad call sounds like).

A *pattern interrupt* certainly helps change the tenor of the call. It has been proven that people will react predictably to certain stimuli. Remember Pavlov's dogs? ***Do the opposite of what salespeople typically do*** and you'll keep the prospect off balance.

Looking for a NO vs. trying to get a sale or an appointment also changes the game. If you see prospecting as a discarding activity, you'll be more likely to ask the hard qualifying questions and you will wind up with well qualified prospects and not people who agreed to see you just because they couldn't get rid of you.

Looking for "pain" as opposed to pitching features and benefits will fundamentally change the way the call is made. Features and benefits are the traditional sales pitch used by 85 percent of salespeople.

The problem with features and benefits is that it fails to differentiate one vendor from another. The promises to save money, reduce downtime and improve customer satisfaction are so overused they become meaningless. Worse, it makes everyone look the same, thereby ***commodotizing*** the product or service.

Finally, it engages the prospect intellectually, not emotionally, and fails to uncover the prospect's problems or pain. The pain approach focuses on the prospect-not the salesperson-and is emotional in concept.

What is the Purpose of Prospecting

If you ask most people in the sales business this question, they will tell you something like "the purpose of prospecting is to get people to give you an appointment. They think if they can make enough appointments and talk to enough people then everything will work out fine. They also will tell you "sales is a numbers game." See enough people and make enough presentations and you will close enough deals. That is so old school. That paradigm went out in the 1970's. Unfortunately, most companies and sales managers still believe and teach that approach. That is why there is so much turnover and failure in the sales profession.

Think about it. If you goal in sales is to talk X number of people and to set Y number of appointments to close Z number of deals, what happens when you fail to achieve that goal? You feel like a lousy, miserable failure. No matter how strong your ego you can only take so much. So what should you do?

Develop a new paradigm that prospecting is the culling out or disqualifying of suspects. If you start trying to disqualify people and you start getting a lot of "NO'S" you are then achieving your goal. You can feel good about yourself. We call this going for the "NO".

> The objective of prospecting is to eliminate those who have no need, no urgency, or no money for your product or service.

Most sales people try to qualify when what they should be doing is trying to disqualify as many suspects as they can. Funny thing is when you adopt this attitude you stop wasting time, become more relaxed and start getting more "Yeses". It really is a paradox.

....

Referral Magic

Perhaps you have sat in an audience watching a sales awards ceremony and been spellbound by the acceptance speeches as the winners talked about their success. If you were struggling at the time, their success may have looked like magic. And you wanted to know how they did it. How did they pull all those sales out of the hat?

The truth is, if their sales came from strong referrals, they may not really know how they did it. Or, they may know what worked and be unwilling to share it. They may want the secrets behind their magic to remain hidden. This is especially true when professionals plan and benefit their referrers exceptionally well. They may want it to look easier than it really was. But you can bet there was much more at play than saying the magic words and just asking for referrals. There was likely a give and take and a sequence of things that happened that made their referral relationships work. There is no real magic that can make the perfect referrals suddenly appear.

The Magic is in Relationships

If you want referrals, you should look past finding which words will work and look instead at what makes relationships work. Referral relationships work like other relationships work. Think about your relationship with people in your neighborhood. Just image the neighbors on your block and their willingness to help you if your car broke down. Each might respond differently, depending on your relationship. One might refuse to help and even be rude. One might share the name of a mechanic. Another might be willing to take you to the garage. And one might be a mechanic and insist on fixing it at no cost. These are very different levels of willingness to help. Your willingness to help would differ for each person, too. Your requests for help would be dependent on your history with each of them and you might not even be sure why you would or wouldn't ask. Your request and their response would be based on a history of mutual benefits. If your request included an offer to benefit them, your request and their response would be based on the anticipation of benefits. But your success would have little to do with how you asked.

"Just asking" is not the Magic

The magic is not in how you ask for referrals. At some level of consciousness, people who sell know the magic is somewhere else. It is true that sometimes just asking for referrals will work. However, the real magic is in the quality of the relationship you have, not the technique you use.

Like a good magic show, successfully getting ideal referrals with strong introductions from influential people involves planning, preparation, and practice. It may look as easy as waving a wand, but the magic is in the building the benefits that result in good relationships. Be sure you do the planning required for your top referrers. The result will be a razzle-dazzle of benefits for you, your referrers, and your new clients!

The Importance of Prospecting

Getting salespeople in front of qualified prospects is typically the number one issue of companies. The ability of the sales force to keep the pipeline full is the key to success.

Without an effective prospecting system in place, the sales pipeline is weak which creates pressure to be more aggressive in selling to poorly qualified prospects. This leads to poor sales, deteriorating margins, frustrated salespeople and concerned management.

Prosper Prospecting Mentality

Prospecting can be equated to *panning for gold*. During the Gold Rush days in California, prospectors set up camp by a stream and patiently sifted through pan after pan of gravel and sand in the hopes of finding a gold nugget or two. It was hard, frustrating work, not unlike sales prospecting today. Perhaps the major difference between the gold prospector and the sales prospector is their attitude toward the process. Gold prospectors knew and accepted that they'd have to go through a great deal of gravel and sand to find a nugget. Instead of being frustrated when most of their effort didn't produce results, they accepted it as the reality of the job.

Unlike the gold prospector, today's salesperson has an unrealistic expectation of prospecting. Instead of accepting the reality that most of their prospecting efforts will be in vain they believe that their prospecting activity should produce significant results. As a result they become frustrated with each call that doesn't pan out.

To prevent disappointment and frustration, salespeople need to change their view of prospecting and remember that ***prospecting is a discarding activity***. The successful salesperson understands that fact and realizes he will need to go through a number of contacts to find the real nugget.

What Keeps You From Prospecting Regularly?

What keeps you from prospecting regularly? A student in one of my classes once answered that question with "just about everything" and there was a loud laughter of recognition from the rest of the students in the class. I mean, they said things like laundry or dishes might even come first. If prospecting is something you'd rather not do, then you must not be having fun with it.

There are two types of prospecting. You can make cold calls or you can call people you know. The highest and best use of your time prospecting is with the people who already trust, know and like you. Yet, I find, most salespeople are not fully leveraging these contacts because they don't want to be seen as pushy. Most of us abhor telemarketers and we think when we are calling to build our business we fall into that category.

Call the people you know and just check in with them. Call to connect, to deepen your relationship. They may not be ready to buy again but they likely have 250 people in their sphere of influence. Staying top-of-mind is the way for them to mention you when they hear of someone thinking of making a purchase.

For fun, just try calling fifteen (15) people a day and have an authentic, friendly conversation. This is even a better exercise to do on one of those days when things aren't going your way and you have crotchety unreasonable people you are dealing with. It will give you an attitude adjustment.

It's the magnetic Principle of Attraction: When you enjoy what you are doing, you attract others by your energy and people want to be around you and refer their friends and family to you. When you are working to do the numbers and are serious about needing business, you repulse and turn people off.

Sometimes, it's time to crank up business we need to stir up the cosmic dust BIG TIME. When that occurs, the more fun you can put in it, the easier it will be to focus and kick some serious butt. Let's take a look at how you are going to approach it.

How about next time you prospect make it your goal to get 15 "no's". Just keep calling until you get those 15 "no's". Do you think if you did that with no attachment to how many "yeses", you should be getting that you might actually get some "yeses"? Now, I don't mean be sloppy about it. What I mean is let go of the outcome and don't take I personally. If they say "no" don't internalize it as personal rejection. It is more about them and where they are at that moment. Your job is just to listen to what they really say and then give it your best shot rather than having your self-worth based on whether or not they agreed to see you. The other useful part of this exercise is honing your skill. So after each call, note in a journal what worked and what didn't. Then on the next call, tweak your approach. Play this game today and realize you win when you get 15 "no's".

As Jimmy Buffet says, "Fun is about the best habit there is."

A Prospecting System That Guarantees Results!

A large majority of salespeople struggle to get in front of enough prospects to keep their pipeline full. As a result, they feel desperate, have a difficult time dealing with rejection, and often avoid asking the tough questions to find out if they really should be spending their time with someone. This leads to a long selling cycle, inefficient time management, and ultimately, failure.

The solution: Make prospecting a game. Here's a great idea to prime your pipeline and put the fun back in prospecting!

The 20 Point Daily Activity System

- 1 point for a telephone contact with a decision maker.

- 1 point for a "customer service" call on an existing client.

- 2 points for forcing a decision to a "NO".

- 2 points for setting an appointment.

- 3 points for getting a referral.

- 4 points for a face-to-face meeting.

- 5 points for a sale.

What makes this work is a management principal that says, "Whatever you track or keep score will improve." Earning points gives you a target that lets you "earn" a reward. You can modify this system to fit your situation if you want, but don't quit until you get your 20 points daily. Your goal becomes getting your 20 points not making sales. This takes all the pressure off of you. When you get your 20 points daily reward yourself at the end of the week. Not only will you make more sales you will also feel good about yourself because you know you are doing the right activity.

(Thanks to our old friend John Condry, Career Success Seminars, for this idea.)

....

When All Else Fails Go To Work

MOST of the people who are in need of what you sell don't even know they have a need. Therefore, they will not seek help on their own. If you are to be successful you must identify your target market and then begin to contact those people. The most effective way is to pick up the phone and call these people to see if they have any interest in talking with someone who does what you do. This approach is not complicated or difficult. The key to being successful in this approach is to have an effective 30 second commercial that identifies 3 to 5 "pains" that you help people fix or improve.

Here is an example:

> "My name is _____. May I take 30 seconds and tell you why I called and you can tell me if you want to talk any further?" (Most people will say OK. Some will not. Don't worry about it. Just hang up and call someone else.)
>
> "I work with clients who are
>
> Frustrated..........
>
> Upset...............
>
> Concerned.........
>
> Angry..............

Once you have completed this ask them "Are any of these things important enough for you to spend two minutes talking about?" (If they say yes continue by asking, "Which of these issues is the most important?" Get them talking and you will help them discover for themselves that they may need what you have.

If you will use this approach you can make 35 dials per hour, contact 5 to 7 people, and make a least one appointment. The beauty of this approach is that it is quick and inexpensive.

CHAPTER 2: ATTITUDES

....

Excellence or Mediocrity

Most salespeople don't treat the profession of selling as a profession. Selling, like medicine or law or accounting requires intensive education and training. Can you imagine going to an accountant or an attorney whose only education was occasionally attending a seminar or reading a book? That is how most salespeople get their training!

I have been in sales for many years and I am proud to call myself a salesperson. Many years ago when I got in this business I "knew that I didn't know". So, I went out and bought some books and began to study. My personal library is full of books, tapes, videos and anything else I can get my hands on to help me learn about this profession. I have attended countless seminars and training programs and have invested literally thousands of hours and dollars on my education.

I don't regret this or bemoan the fact that I did this. I simply did what I had to do to become excellent at my chosen profession. If one desires to have income this is what it takes. On the other hand, if mediocrity is acceptable then these things are not necessary.

Focusing On the Wrong End of The Problem

Many of the questions I get asked by salespeople tend to be "how to" or "technique" type questions. These questions are most often the wrong questions to be asking. Why?

Because only about twenty percent (20%) of sales success can be attributed to technique(s). Simply put, asking technique type questions focuses on the wrong end of the problem. That focus is one reason that most sales training doesn't work. Selling is not about what you do. It is about who you are. We have known for years that our belief system is far more important than any technique(s) we use. Belief has to do with belief about product, market, company, competition and, most importantly, belief about our self. According to psychologist Denis Waitley, who has been a psychologist for the U.S. Olympic teams, "we don't get what we want in life but we do get what we expect."

Selling, like life, is a self-fulfilling prophecy. Instead of harping on "how to", we should be asking ourselves why am I having these problems? What beliefs are getting in the way of my success? What self-limiting beliefs do I need to change? If this sounds a bit like therapy that's because it is. To be truly successful in life we have to be honest with ourselves and be willing to change. Sadly, most people don't have the guts to confront their own "head trash".

There is a rule of human nature that says: "You can only perform in your role in sales or life in a manner that is consistent with how you see yourself performing." What you visualize you materialize. That's what Napoleon Hill wrote about in "Think and Grow Rich". The key word being "Think".

Whatever circumstances you and I are experiencing at this moment are because of the way we think.

And what we think is ultimately our own responsibility. We can't blame the economy, the competition, our company, the industry, 9/11/01 or anything else for what we think.

··

Only Decision Makers Can Get Others to Make Decisions

According to Dave Kurlan, author of *Mindless Selling* and developer of the Dave Kurlan Sales Profile, there are five major weaknesses that impact success in selling. The most powerful of those is Buy Cycle.

According to Kurlan, "Buy Cycle refers to the process by which salespeople make purchases for themselves."

Because salespeople use the same paradigm for buying and selling they will tolerate behavior from their prospects when it is similar and consistent to their own. A Buy Cycle that fails to align itself with an ideal selling process causes many of the obstacles that salespeople are unable to handle effectively.

For instance, a salesperson who is a "comparison shopper" when it comes to spending their money will tolerate the same behavior from their prospect because subconsciously it makes sense to do so. Same thing with "I Want to Think It Over". A non-supportive Buy Cycle also makes salespeople more vulnerable to stalls, put offs, lies, excuses, sob stories, procrastinators, price shoppers and researchers.

Salespeople with this weakness agree with the prospect's reasons for wishing to think things over. Therefore, the prospect's wish is granted, business is either lost or delayed, and the salesperson wastes a tremendous amount of time performing unnecessary follow-up.

Despite attempts to tell or train salespeople what they should do in these situations, they continue to say or do things that don't achieve the desired outcome. Why? Because they cannot escape their own internal programming.

The only solution to this problem is for salespeople to change the way they make purchases. This is not some technique to be learned in any class. This is about personal CHANGE. When salespeople change their Buy Cycles to support the selling process, the stalls and put-offs that used to derail their process will become momentary delays in a single sales call.

One of the most successful characteristics of high performance individuals is their ability to make decisions. Learn to become a decision maker because only decision makers can get others to make decisions. Your role as a salesperson is to get the prospect to say either "Yes I Do or No I Don't". You can only do this if you BECOME that kind of person yourself.

....

Need for Approval

Need for approval is one of the major weaknesses that a salesperson can have. Not only is it a powerful weakness, it is the most difficult one to overcome.

What are the consequences of Need For Approval? When the need to be liked is great, salespeople won't ask people to make decisions. Salespeople who have this issue will not close effectively. They will find it difficult to ask tough questions because they're afraid that their prospects may become upset. They tend to be non-confrontational. They will waste time with prospects that lie rather than ask prospects why they are being misled. They are likely to accept "maybes" instead of "no's" because to them a "no" means that they didn't get their prospect's approval. And they will waste time and have an unnecessarily longer sell cycle!

Salespeople who suffer from need for approval need to be reminded on a daily basis that it doesn't matter what prospects think or say about them.

What they need to do is to get their prospects to respect them rather than needing their prospects to like them.

While this weakness will affect a salesperson's ability to close, it is also a frequent companion to the prospecting component of selling. A salesperson with this weakness often suffers from call reluctance and fear of rejection.

Overcoming Need for Approval

Wanting the approval of other people is a natural human condition. We all like emotional strokes and positive affirmations from others. It is only when this want becomes a "need" does it begin to interfere with sales success. If you have a need for approval it will affect you by getting in your way at the most inappropriate times. Most often, it will inhibit your ability to ask questions, confront when necessary, close for appointments and sales, recover from rejection and really enjoy selling.

Overcome it by changing your mind-set.

Selling is not a place to get your emotional needs met.

It is simply an arena in which commerce is conducted. The most successful salespeople are those who approach sales from an emotionally detached point of view. They approach selling with the same emotional detachment that a surgeon approaches surgery.

Here are six steps that we teach to help clients overcome the Need For Approval:

1. Identify the self-limiting beliefs that get in the way. Here are some examples: I can't confront a prospect. I can't ask questions that might upset a prospect. There are certain things that you just can't say to prospects. It's rude to ask a lot of personal questions. I am uncomfortable asking prospects about their budget.

2. Replace these beliefs with new beliefs like: I am comfortable confronting prospects in a nurturing way. Prospects don't get upset when I ask good, nurturing questions. I can say anything to anybody as long as I say it nicely. I love to ask personal questions. I enjoy discussing money with prospects.

3. Rewrite these new beliefs on index cards and carry them with you. At every chance you get during the day, pull them

out and read them out loud. Do this every morning and just before you go to bed each night.

4. Find a tape recorder and a 60-minute tape. Record these new records in your own voice, over, and over until you've filled both sides of the tape.

5. Begin listening to the tape at least once per day for six weeks. After a few weeks you will begin to notice a difference in your self-talk.

6. Read "Your Erroneous Zones" by Dr. Wayne Dyer.

....

All for Twenty Dollars

A well-known speaker started off his seminar by holding up a twenty-dollar bill. In a room of two hundred he asked, "who would like this twenty dollar bill?"

Hands started going up. He said, "I am going to give this twenty-dollar bill to one of you but first let me do this." He proceeded to crumple the bill up. He then asked, "who still wants it"? Still the hands were up in the air.

Well, he replied, "what if I do this?" And he dropped it on the ground and started to grind it into the floor with his shoe. He then picked it up, crumpled and dirty. Now "who still wants it?" Still the hands went up.

"My friends, we have all learned a very valuable lesson. No matter what I did to the money, you still wanted it because it did not decrease in value. It is still worth twenty dollars".

"Many times in our lives we are dropped, crumpled, and ground into the dirt by the decisions we make and the circumstances that come our way. We feel as though we are worthless. But no matter what has happened or what will happen, you will never lose your value: dirty or clean, crumpled or finely creased, you are still priceless to those who love you. The worth of our lives comes not in what we do or what we have or who we know but by WHO WE ARE".

You are special – don't EVER forget it. And remember to count your blessings not your problems.

....

I Couldn't Sleep Last Night

I woke up thinking about what I am doing and why I am doing it. My mind would not let go of the question, "why are some people enormously successful while others seem to struggle to find clients." So I sit here at 2:55 am journaling my thoughts.

I don't understand why selling is so hard for people, because it has never been hard for me. Obtaining clients has always been easy for me when I did the prospecting behavior.

Why is that?

I think it is because I am so convicted about what I do and why I do it that it is impossible for someone to attend one of my classes, or to spend time with me, without coming away with the impression that I believe in and am passionate about what I am saying and doing. They may not become a client, but they sure do believe that I believe in what I am doing. I have always believed, even when I struggled financially.

Where does this belief come from?

It comes from the fact that I am I engaged in an affair of the heart, and I that I love what I do. Teaching and training people and watching them grow and develop new skills has been a passion for me since, as a sixteen year old lifeguard, I first experienced the thrill of teaching two year old babies how to swim.

I am doing what God created me to do and it comes easily for me.

What is your primary reason for doing what you are doing?

If it is only to make money, you will never become fabulously successful. You will struggle and never find true happiness and peace of mind.

Why are you here? What is your life purpose? Are you trying to do your will or God's will?

These are some powerful questions that beg answers. The answers to these and other equally important questions are buried deeply inside of you. If you want to find the answers, you must become deeply introspective and get real with yourself.

Truly, successful and happy people have spent a great deal of time answering these questions. They know who they are and why they are here. They know their strengths and their limitations. They accept both of them for what they are and they don't wish or try to become someone else. They are content, but not satisfied and they don't covet others gifts or success. They are very rare individuals indeed.

Are you one of these people or do you find that life is a grind and a daily struggle?

If you are not consumed with passion or have a burning desire to do what you are now doing, quit immediately and go do what you are passionate about. You owe it to yourself, your family and to mankind to pursue what God meant for you to do. Until you do this, you will, in Henry David Thoreau's words, be among the "mass of men who lead lives of quiet desperation".

It Is Not How You Feel That Determines How You Act.

"It is not how you feel that determines how you act.
It is how you act that determines how you feel"...

....said William James the famous Harvard Psychologist.

"If you want to change your emotional state, change your physiology", says Tony Robbins.

Faith and Fear cannot exist in the same mind at the same time. If one has a good plan and executes consistently, then they don't have time to feel miserable.

If you find yourself feeling down then get up and "do something". It will make you feel better even if you get no results.

However, if you have a good plan and execute consistently, then you will get great results. If you do this you will be ahead of your competitors when the economy turns around. The economy *WILL* turn and those who are faithfully doing the right things now will be the beneficiaries.

Coming to Terms: 21st Century Demands

The popular stereotype of the career salesperson is still shaped by the image of Arthur Miller's Willy Loman. You remember Willy, the doomed hero of the play *Death of a Salesman,* whose livelihood seemed to depend, for most of his career, on smiling relentlessly, slapping backs, keeping his shoes shined and striving endlessly to be "well-liked".

Interestingly, Willie Loman never once spoke in Miller's play of how his customers actually used his product or even what his product was! Who needed information like that? In his prime, Willy could apparently charm customers into submission.

The media's image of the professional salesperson, by and large, is still that of the fast-talking "company person" who takes over conversations, presents a relentlessly smooth image to prospects and customers, delivers a generally unvarying sales pitch and cheerfully takes down orders. Whether or not this model was appropriate during the 1940s and 1950s, it's certainly not appropriate today.

There is every indication that today's highly competitive, technologically driven economy will, in the years to come, leave less and less room for salespeople who have fallen behind the times. Those are salespeople who fail to adopt a consultative, information-centered approach to their work are likely to find their career prospects very dim indeed.

The salespeople who prosper, or survive, in the economy of this new century will assume responsibility for in-depth account development with their prospects and customers. They will focus not on the shallow "numbers game" of selling that requires little or no interviewing skill, but rather on asking questions and gathering more pertinent facts than the competition about the experience, objectives and history of their prospects and customers.

Regardless of the products or services you hope to sell, if you wish to succeed as a salesperson in the 21st century, you must be sure that your work is geared toward asking the truly thoughtful questions that set the stage for the most appropriate product/service offering. Although such a goal seems to reflect simple common sense, it is ignored by a huge number of salespeople and, indeed, by most of the traditional selling strategies used in formal and informal corporate sales training.

....

How To Become A Top Performer

1. **Set Goals** –Set annual, monthly, and weekly income and revenue goals. Identify what and how much sales activity must be done weekly, monthly and annually to achieve those goals. Commit to the activity and set up a method of tracking and keeping score daily. (It is not hard to do this. But you do have to THINK!)

2. **Visualize and Dream** – Create a dream board by cutting out pictures of what you desire and pasting them on a sheet of poster board. Take trips to see houses, cars boats, etc. Put yourself mentally in those places and begin to visualize what it will look like and feel like when you are living that dream. Develop a written description of the person you want to become.

3. **Read and Study Daily** – Commit to learn everything you can about psychology, sales and human nature. Read at least 30 minutes per day in one of these areas. At that level you can read at least one book a month. Did you know that 90% of all the sales books bought each year are bought by 10% of the salespeople? Guess which 10%. There is a correlation.

4. **Listen to Audio Tape/CD programs** – The average sales rep spends hundreds of hours each year behind the wheel of their car. Turn that time into a learning experience. Turn off the radio and listen to something that will help you make money. Set a goal to listen to one new Tape/CD program each month.

5. **Journal and Debrief** – Keep a journal and debrief ALL of your sales calls. That way you can reinforce what you did right and learn what you need to differently the next time. I you do this you will become your own best sales coach. Don't expect your manager to do this for you. It is your life not theirs.

Stuck In A Comfort Zone

All of us experience a "comfort zone" from time to time. This is a natural part of the human experience. That is not the problem. The problem is not recognizing or being aware or knowing what to do when we are in a comfort zone. How do we recognize and avoid the natural tendency to get stuck in a comfort zone?

Recognize the Trap

Look back over your past experiences and identify those times in your life when your performance leveled off for no apparent reason. Is there a pattern A person in a comfort zone tends to feel tense and uneasy about change, or even the thought of change. Emerson said, "A foolish consistency is the hobgoblin of little minds." You can overcome the tendency to stay trapped in a comfort zones by first recognizing it in yourself and then by observing it in others.

Analyze Your Behavior

In the past when you found yourself in a comfort zone did you push through it or did you change course to avoid the discomfort of change?

Keep an Open Mind

Remember, a hallmark of high achievers people is an open mind on all subjects, the willingness to listen carefully and patiently, without prejudgment or jumping to conclusions.

Learn From Your Mistakes

Fear of failure, of being wrong, of making a mistake keeps people from risking and trying to break out of their comfort zone. Probably 80 percent or more of adults are so worried about being wrong that they shy away from any risky situation.

Set Goals And Take Action

Develop and visualize clearly goals and objectives. Goals create passion. Without passion we become complacent and begin a downward spiral towards mediocrity. This leads to self-doubt and erosion of our self worth.

Commit To Excellence

Commit to reaching the highest levels of your potential. Each time you break through a comfort zone and achieve a higher level of performance set new goals. Look at your comfort zone as a motivator, not a barrier. Breaking through your comfort zone leads you to higher and higher levels of accomplishment and brings exhilaration and increased self worth.

The Five Stages Of Sales Mastery

Stage One – Unconscious Incompetent

This is the stage where you are oblivious. It could be said, "You don't know that you don't know". At this stage you are unaware and unskilled.

Stage Two – Conscious Incompetent

This is the stage where you become aware that you are unskilled. At this stage you come to "know that you don't know" that your skills are lacking. This can be very uncomfortable and perhaps intimidating.

Stage Three – Conscious Competent

This is the stage where you are becoming more skilled and comfortable with the new behaviors or skills. It seems like hard work because you have to "think about" everything you are doing. It requires a lot of mental energy and can be exhausting. At this stage you are beginning to "get the hang of it".

Stage Four – Unconscious Competent

This is the stage where you can execute "in the moment". You no longer have to think about your response to any situation. You are running on autopilot. You now own the new behavior or skill. It usually takes two to five years of constant practice and study to get to this stage. Less than 10% of sales people ever achieve this level.

Stage Five- Master

This is the stage where you begin to develop new skills, attitudes and behaviors that have not yet been taught or discovered. You become a guru or pioneer. Less than 2% of sales people ever reach this level. It takes five to ten years of intense study to reach this level.

Ghosts, Goblins and the Boogey Man—Be careful who you listen to

Hysteria is running rampant in the news media. Headlines like these are filling the front pages of newspapers and news magazines across the country.

"*Economists bet housing prices will fall 10% more*"

"*Homebuilder Lennar Corp posts third-quarter loss of $510 million and cut its work force by 35%.*"

"It's going to be a distressingly long time before we get back to normal."

"The National Association of Realtors reported existing home salesl fell in August to the lowest level in five years."

"Nearly 180,000 homes fell into foreclosure in July, up 93 percent from a year ago."

"Sales of new single-family homes were off 22.3 percent in June from a year earlier."

"The National Association of Realtors reports there's enough housing inventory for sale to last 9.6 months, more than double the 2005 level."

"This is the largest sustained decline in year-over-year prices since 1991," says Yale economist Robert Shiller.

"The collateral damage is spreading."

"The second quarter, same-store sales were down 5.2 percent at Home Depot and 4.3 percent at Sears."

"In July, auto sales were down 12 percent from the year before."

"The sky is falling. The sky is falling". NOT.

Relax. We have been here many times before.

When Jimmy Carter was President in the 1970s we had double digit inflation, double digit interest rates (400% higher than today)- my home mortgage was 13%- and double digit unemployment, gas lines and gas rationing. All of this led to an avalanche of home foreclosures and the collapse of savings and loans banks.

In the 1980s and again in 1991 we had a recession. No big deal just an economic bump in the road that preceded one of the greatest bull markets the world has ever seen.

If the financial hysteria doesn't scare you how about lead poisoned toys, fish and tea from China, global warming, the melting of the polar ice cap, the bird flu epidemic, terrorist plots, the war in Iraq, the sub prime debacle. Pick your boogey man. To quote Jimmy Buffet, "It's a scary world out there kiddies."

In its desperate need to fill the airways and tabloids the mass media manufactures hysteria, dire predictions and over hyped crisis that scares the hell out of a jaded, uniformed and ignorant public. They do that because they know if they were to report on the low unemployment rates, low interest rates and a healthy economy they wouldn't draw much of a crowd.

While there is a significant correction in the bloated housing market - remember the talk of a housing bubble just three years ago and the stock market correction earlier in this decade - we are not headed for an economic depression. Recession maybe. Depression not a chance.

The key to your prosperity in good times and in bad is to eliminate a scarcity mentality by learn to focus on Cultivating an Abundant Mentality. If you will do this you will position yourself to take advantage of the fear and hysteria that permeates the business landscape?

At some point you have to decide who you are going to listen to.

Are you going to cower in a corner like a small child and let the talking network heads tell you what your future will be or are you going to grow up and take personal responsibility for your own thoughts, actions and destiny?

Most of the talking heads that are making noise are simply making noise. There is no real basis for their mindless chatter. They sit and stare at the little red light on top of the television camera and pontificate as if they have a crystal ball and can foretell the future. They can't. I can't and neither can you or anyone else.

The business reality is that people are still buying stuff and spending money. Lots of money. People are still eating at restaurants, going to movie theaters and shopping at the malls. People are still buying insurance, houses, cars and clothing and they are still traveling to exotic vacation destinations. Businesses are still buying advertising, computers, office furniture and everything else businesses normally buy.

The bottom line is that people are still buying the stuff you or your company sells. They may not be buying quite as much or spending quite as recklessly as they were but they are still spending trillions of dollars annually.

As I survey my clients across the U.S. and Canada, I find a common theme. Those companies who are excellent at what they do, have a clear vision, a detailed plan, and aggressively go after market share are growing their sales revenues and profits by double digits.

Those who are slovenly, unfocused, half committed and operationally mediocre are struggling or shrinking now that the easy money has disappeared.

Let's face it. When times are easy anyone can make money. **When things tighten up we find out who the real players are.**

The beautiful thing about the market is that it always separates those who are performers from those who are pretenders. This shaking out process that culls, cleanses and prunes the market of business imposters is healthy.

Today's economic climate is not a negative. It is a great opportunity to leap ahead of your competition and become the dominate player in your market.

Are you excellent at what you do? Do you have a clear vision and written goals? Do you have a detailed written plan to achieve your goals? Are you aggressively going after market share?

BE THANKFUL FOR WHAT WE HAVE

If we could shrink the earth's population to a village of precisely 100 people, with all the existing human ratios remaining the same, it would look something like the following. There would be:

- 57 Asians

- 21 Europeans

- 14 from the Western Hemisphere, both north and south

- 8 Africans

- 52 would be female

- 48 would be male

- 70 would be non-white

- 30 would be white

- 70 would be non-Christian

- 30 would be Christian

- 89 would be heterosexual

- 11 would be homosexual

- 6 people would possess 59% of the entire world's wealth and all 6 would be from the United States

- 80 would live in substandard housing

- 70 would be unable to read

- 50 would suffer from malnutrition

- 1 would be near death; 1 would be near birth

- 1 (yes, only 1) would have a college education

- 1 would own a computer

When one considers our world from such a compressed perspective, the need for acceptance, understanding and education becomes glaringly apparent.

The following is also something to ponder:

If you woke up this morning with more health than illness...you are more blessed than one million who will not survive this week.

If you have never experienced the danger of battle, the loneliness of imprisonment, the agony of torture, or the pangs of starvation...you are ahead of 500 million people in the world.

If you can attend a church meeting without the fear of harassment, arrest, torture or death...you are more blessed than three billion people in the world.

If you have food in the refrigerator, clothes on your back, a roof overhead and a place to sleep…you are richer than 75% of this world.

If you have money in the bank, in your wallet, and spare change in a dish someplace…you are among the top 8% of the world's wealthy.

If your parents are still alive and still married…you are very rare, even in the United States and Canada.

If you can read this message, you just received a double blessing in that someone was thinking of you, and furthermore, you are more blessed than over two billion people in the world that cannot read at all.

Someone once said: *What goes around comes around.*

> *Work like you don't need the money.*
>
> *Love like you've never been hurt.*
>
> *Dance like nobody's watching.*
>
> *Sing like nobody's listening.*
>
> *Live like it's Heaven on Earth.*

....

Happiness Is A Learned Skill

We live in a time of great opportunity and in a country where there is so much possibility. Yet a great number of people are living in misery. Psychic distress is rampant. Mental health clinics are inundated and anti depressant use is at an all time high.

Why are so many people so unhappy?

Part of the reason can be found by analyzing people's expectations. All of us have visions or images of how things should be in our lives. We tend to base our emotions on "how things are going versus how we think they should be going". When there is great disparity between the two we become frustrated. Only when our expectations and our reality are integrated and in sync can we be happy.

We see this happing in selling all the time. Here is how it works. Sales people who expect to close every deal or who expect that most prospects are going to welcome them with open arms become highly frustrated, upset and angry when their experience doesn't match their expectation. As a result, they begin to internalize this experience as personal failure. Confidence and self-image begins to suffer. If this isn't corrected it often leads to an early exit from the profession.

So what's the answer?

Instead of measuring and comparing yourself against someone else or the ideal or your view of perfection compare yourself with yourself. Analyze and measure how much progress you have made. By using the past as a benchmark you can see the progress you have made. As you begin to see your progress and experience more personal victories and a greater sense of self-confidence. Instead of constantly feeling that you have failed you will experience more happiness and begin to celebrate the many little victories that you have. What a great way to live.

....

Positioning Your Business
in This Crazy Market

I have been invited to give a keynote speech "Positioning Your Business in This Crazy Market" to a group of 150 Las Vegas business owners. Here is a sneak preview of what you would hear if you were in this audience.

I would start off telling you that the business fruit you are now harvesting is the result of many years of cultivation or neglect and that there are no secrets to learn or magic potions to drink or fairy dust that can be sprinkled on you that will change that.

The tough reality is that the business of growing a business is a long hard up hill slog and the sooner you get busy doing the things that successful businesses do the sooner you will reap more abundant and delicious fruit.

You might be wondering where I would tell you to start.

I would tell you to focus on three key areas:

Business Strategy and Leadership Skills

I would tell you to analyze your self and be honest about your leadership skills, business strategy and acumen. If you have the courage and self honesty to confront and examine your leadership skills, business acumen and strategy and attitudes there is hope. If you are not willing to do that you might as well close the doors because your business is already dead.

Every business owners business is a reflection of the owner's skills, attitudes, and competency.

The health of a business is not a reflection of the economy or market conditions or industry trends. It is a personal reflection of the owner's business skills. Period!

Successful business owners understand and accept this.

The World Inside Their Business

I would tell you to make sure your house is in order before you invite people to come visit. Having your house in order means more than having an attractive and clean physical plant. It means having policies and procedures that make it easy and fun for customers to do business with you; it means having friendly and helpful employees who have a servant attitude and truly enjoy their work.

I would tell you that you need to improve your employee selection and retention process by benchmarking each position and by investing the time, money and energy necessary to hire the best people available. I would tell you that you need to invest heavily in ongoing communication and sales skills training of all of your staff. None of these things will be cheap, easy or quick. The alternative is to do nothing and hope for the best. Unfortunately, hope is not a good strategy.

The World Outside Your Business

I would tell you that you are not in the retail business or the automotive or computer or plumbing or florist or any other business you may think you are in but that *you are in the marketing business* and you need to learn how to become marketing experts. You would hear that you need to learn to become students of marketing and that you need to quit relying on so called marketing experts who are merely advertising sales people. You would hear that you need to determine what your Unique Selling Proposition is and then you need to craft effective copy to communicate that message. Lastly and only when you have done the previous two things do you need to worry about which media you need to use to effectively communicate your message

Additionally, you would hear that you need to learn to become better direct response marketers and that you need to stay away from image building or marketing that you can't measure or quantify.

You would hear that you need to become involved in your community and begin to volunteer your time and energy to a cause that you are passionate about.

All of these things will require that you invest more time, energy and money in your business. If you are unwillingly to do that then you need to either learn to be happy with your current results or you need to seriously consider doing something else.

....

Is It Real or Is It Imagined

Liu Chi Kung, a world-class pianist in the late 1950's was imprisoned during the Cultural Revolution in China. After seven years without a piano he immediately resumed his concert tour. His fans said he played better than ever and wondered how this was possible. Kung said, "I rehearsed every piece I had ever played, note by note, in my mind."

Psychological research has proven that the mind cannot neurologically tell the difference between a real occurrence and one that has been imagined. The moment you experience an event vividly in your imagination it is neurologically recorded as a "real experience".

Mental rehearsal,or the process of visualization creates new neurological pathways in the brain and can give you a competitive edge. Olympic athletes have used it in training for years and it works not only in sports but also in business, education and anything else we do.

Unfortunately, this also works to our detriment. When we visualize failure or losing a sale the brain records this as "real" and our subconscious goes about making this a reality. We cannot control the process but we can control what we visualize and think about.

So the next time you make a phone call, schedule an important appointment, or make a sales presentation, practice positive mental rehearsal beforehand. You can think your way to success. You don't need any special tools, it doesn't cost anything, and you can begin right now. Imagine that!

Ten Principles Of Subconscious Programming

1. The human brain is a physiological organ which, through a specific electrochemical process, collects, processes, stores, and acts on information it receives.

2. Information presented to the subconscious mind triggers both a physiological response and psychological response.

3. Any information presented to the subconscious mind is always linked to, and affected by, previously stored information.

4. The subconscious mind is a <u>neutral</u> mechanism which responds to information without subjective regard for its action.

5. The subconscious mind holds no beliefs or biases other than those which it receives as a result of its programming.

6. When faced with two or more programs that are in conflict with each other, the subconscious will attempt to act on the program which is strongest.

7. The strength of the program is influenced by the number of times the same or similar information is presented.

8. The strength of the program is influenced by the perceived importance of the program source.

9. The strength of the program is influenced by the amount of emotion associated with the program.

10. The subconscious mind will, at all times, attempt to act on its dominate operative program.

The Carpenter

An elderly carpenter was ready to retire. He told his employer-contractor of his plans to leave the house-building business and live a more leisurely life with his wife enjoying his extended family. He would miss the paycheck, but he needed to retire. They could get by. The contractor was sorry to see his good worker go and asked if he could build just one more house as a personal favor. The carpenter said yes, but in time it was easy to see that his heart was not in his work. He resorted to shoddy workmanship and used inferior materials. It was an unfortunate way to end a dedicated career.

When the carpenter finished his work the employer came to inspect the house. He handed the front-door key to the carpenter. "This is your house," he said, "my gift to you."

The carpenter was shocked! What a shame! If he had only known he was building his own house, he would have done it all so differently.

Sot it is with us. We build our lives, a day at a time, often putting less that our best into the building. Then with a shock we realize we have to live in the house we have built. If we could do it over, we'd do it much differently.

But we cannot go back. You are the carpenter. Each day you hammer a nail, place a board, or erect a wall.

"Life is a do-it-yourself project," someone has said.

Your attitudes and the choices you make today, build the "house" you live in tomorrow. Build wisely!

....

Who You Are Does Make A Difference

A teacher in New York decided to honor each of her seniors in high school by telling them the difference they each made. She called each student to the front of the class, one at a time.

First she told each one of them how they had made a difference to her and to the class. Then she presented each of them with a blue ribbon imprinted with gold letters, which read, "Who I Am Makes a Difference."

Afterwards the teacher decided to do a class project to see what kind of impact recognition would have on a community. She gave each of the students three more ribbons and instructed them to go out and spread this acknowledgment ceremony. They were to follow up on the results, see who honored whom and report back to the class in about a week.

One of the boys in the class went to a junior executive in a nearby company and honored him for helping him with his career planning. He gave him a blue ribbon and put it on his shirt. Then he gave him two extra ribbons and said, "We're doing a class project on recognition, and we'd like you to go out, find somebody to honor, give them a blue ribbon, then give them the extra blue ribbon so they can acknowledge a third person to keep this acknowledgment ceremony going. Then please report back to me and tell me what happened.

Later that day the junior executive went in to see his boss, who had been noted, by the way, as being kind of a grouchy fellow. He sat down with his boss and he told him that he deeply admired him for being a creative genius. The boss seemed very surprised. The junior executive asked him if he would accept the gift of the blue ribbon and would he give him permission to put it on him. His surprised boss said, "Well, sure." The junior executive took the blue ribbon and placed it right on his boss's jacket above his heart. As he gave him the extra ribbon, he said, "Would you do me a favor? Would you take this extra ribbon and pass it on by honoring somebody else." The young boy who first gave me the ribbons is doing a project in school and we want to keep this recognition ceremony going and find out how it affects people.

That night the boss came home to his 14-year-old son and sat him down. He said, "The most incredible thing happened to me today. I was in my office and one of the junior executives came in and told me he admired me and gave me a blue ribbon for being a creative genius. Imagine, He thinks I'm a creative genius. Then he put this blue ribbon that says, "Who I Am Makes a Difference" on my jacket above my heart. He gave me the extra ribbon and asked me to find somebody else to honor. As I was driving home tonight, I started thinking about whom I would honor with this ribbon and I thought about you. I want to honor you.

My days are really hectic and when I come home I don't pay a lot of attention to you. Sometimes I scream at you for not getting good enough grades in school and for your bedroom being a mess, but somehow tonight, I just wanted to sit here and, well, just let you know that you do make a difference to me. Besides your mother, you are the most important person in my life. You're a great kid and I love you.

The startled boy started to sob and sob, and he couldn't stop crying. His whole body shook. He looked up at his father and said through his tears, "Dad, earlier tonight I sat in my room and wrote a letter to you and Mom explaining why I had killed myself and asking you to forgive me. I was going to commit suicide tonight after you were asleep. I just didn't think you cared at all. The letter is upstairs. I don't think I need it after all.

His father walked upstairs and found a heartfelt letter full of anguish and pain. The envelope was addressed, "Mom and Dad".

The boss went back to work a changed man. He was no longer a grouch but made sure to let all his employees know that they made a difference. The junior executive helped several other young people with career planning and never forgot to let them know that they made a difference in his life...one being the boss's son. The young boy and his classmates learned a valuable lesson.

Who you are **DOES** make a difference! Start letting the people who matter to you know that they make a difference to you.

CHAPTER 3: QUALIFYING

How Much Info Should You Give Away In A Proposal?

If you have to ask the question, you are headed down the wrong track. If you give away your knowledge in a written proposal before the prospect has committed to give you a yes or no decision, you are setting yourself up to lose. Failure to do this will almost certainly produce an "I want to think it over" response from the prospect. At that point you have just been "rolled" and have become victim of free consulting. After all, when the prospect has all of your information why do they need you?

To avoid this what should you do? Only deal with prospects with which you can quickly develop a relationship of mutual trust and respect. These are people who need, want, and can afford your services and are willing to buy from you. When there is mutual trust and respect, the prospect will share information, and make commitments to do business with you if you can meet his or her conditions of satisfaction. These conditions are agreed upon before any work is done or any analysis or proposal is generated. Before any proposal is generated the prospect must decide that you are the person they want to work with. Instead of closing at the end of the proposal process you are, in effect, closing up front.

Before the prospect buys your product or service they must first buy you. As you work with the prospect to mutually decide on the solution to their problems and the costs associated with the solution, the proposal will verbally evolve by mutual agreement. Prospects with whom you have a relationship of mutual trust and respect will be honest about this process.

Prospects who refuse to be honest and try to make you jump through hoops, like some trained animal, simply are not worth the effort.

The best thing you can do when you encounter them is to disqualify them quickly and move on to prospects that will be real. This is not easy or natural. It requires a lot of courage and training to do this consistently.

Let Me "Think It Over"

Face the facts. You know the most "Think It Overs" are really "nos". That being the case, why not get the "no" early instead of late in the process. To do this you must get rid of the "head trash" that says you've got to try to sell everybody. That is not going to happen. You and I both know that.

Let's look at the problems with "Think It Overs". It allows our prospect to steal your valuable information and "shop it around". It allows the prospect to control the sales process. It results in unrealistic pipeline and forecasting (how much of your current forecast is bogus). It gives you a false sense of security and when it becomes apparent that there will not be a deal it's devastating emotionally. What's the answer?

Here are two suggestions. First, make sure your initial agreement covers the fact that at the end of the first meeting that there needs to be a mutual agreement between you and the prospect about specifically what happens next, when it is going to happen and what decisions will be made at the next meeting.

Secondly, develop the mindset that your prospect must convince you that there is a reason for your continued involvement in the sales process. In other words, if you're having any doubts that the two of you should continue the process, tell the prospect. Then let him convince you why you should stay involved. The prospect must convince you not vice versa. This takes courage. Unfortunately, most salespeople don't have it.

....

To Qualify or Disqualify

What's the difference between qualifying and disqualifying and how is it accomplished? I'm assuming we are talking about someone who might be interested in what you have to offer.

It is all in the mindset. Qualifying implies that the salesperson is looking to "qualify" the prospect as someone they might try to sell to. In this case the salesperson is the one doing the selling. Disqualifying is just the opposite. The salesperson is looking for every reason to stop the selling process. This makes the prospect the one that has to sell the salesperson on continuing the sales process.

This is accomplished by following a systematic process which the salesperson controls and which the prospect must be willing to submit. If the prospect fails to follow the process, or fights the salesperson for control of the process or refused to answer the salespersons questions, then the salesperson disqualifies them. The smart salesperson knows that at any given time only about 5 – 10% of the people they talk to will end up becoming a client. They don't fight this. They just learn to "cull" people quickly and move on.

How Much Does It Cost
To Give A Proposal

Most salespeople think that the key to sales success is to relentlessly and persistently get in front of as many prospects as possible and to present proposals to anyone who is willing to listen. Ignorant and misguided sales managers reinforce this mindset by pressuring salespeople to give more proposals and present more solutions. This throw a lot of mud on the wall and see how much sticks approach results in salespeople wasting tons of their time, having a low closing percentages, experiencing massive amounts of rejection and frustration, hours of wasted staff time preparing proposals that never close, lousy sales forecasting, poor staff morale, high sales staff turnover and a myriad of other problems.

The key to eliminating these problems requires a fundamental mindset change on the part of the owners and managers about selling. This mindset change is more than positive thinking. It requires the managers and owners to ruthlessly analyze their beliefs and attitudes about what works and what doesn't, what can and cannot be done and how much they are willing to change the way they do business. The reality is that the problems that are being experienced within the company relative to the sales process are merely a reflection of the owners and managers skills attitudes and beliefs about selling. Only when the owners and managers change their mindset and attitude will there be a change in the sales force.

Managers, owners and salespeople need to analyze how much it cost them to prepare a proposal. When I asked business owners, managers and salespeople how much it cost to prepare a proposal, most of them looked at me as if I'm speaking a foreign language. Not only do they not know the answer to the question, they have never even considered the question. They are blindly following their approach because they've never taken the time to stop and think about this issue.

Recently in a coaching session, I dug deep into this rabbit hole with a client by asking how much time and money was invested to get to the proposal step? Their answer was, "I don't know". I continued to probe further by asking, "Including driving time to and from the appointments how much time has been invested meeting with this prospect"? "Based on how much your time is worth per hour how much do you personally have invested at this point"? Who else besides you has been involved in presenting or preparing this proposal"? "How many hours of their time have been involved putting the proposal together"? Based on their hourly pay scale how many dollars does that represent"? How much has it cost your company in payroll for these people to prepare the proposal for you"? "When you add up everyone's time how much did it cost your company to prepare and present this proposal"? "How many times each week or each month is your company doing this"? "On a monthly basis what is the cost of preparing proposals"? "What percentage of these proposals end up closing"?

When I forced them to give me answers to these questions they were shocked with their answers. They had never considered the cost of going to market. They simply considered giving proposals and hoping for the best the excepted way of doing business in their industry. Doing what everyone else in the industry does is a sure prescription for mediocrity at best and failure at worst. In order to excel and thrive, businesses must do something different than everyone else in their industry. Failure to do that reduces your company offering to a commodity and gives the perception that you're no different than anyone else.

Qualify or Disqualify Early

Most salespeople operate from an entirely self-destructive paradigm.

They operate with the mistaken belief that it is their job to present proposals and quotes to any potential buyer that requests that they do so. They unilaterally give proposals and quotes without requiring the buyer to make any commitments or decisions. They willingly give away free and proprietary information in hopes that the buyer may commit to doing business together. They make no requirement of the buyer to do anything at all once they received the proposal. The end result for the sellers are huge numbers of put offs, stalls and think it over's.

To prevent this from happening sellers must have the courage and fortitude to extract commitments and obligations from the buyers in order to receive a proposal, quote or presentation. No other profession willingly gives away free information at no cost or no obligation to their customers. Attorneys don't give free advice. CPAs don't give free advice. Physicians don't give free advice. Only salespeople give free advice in hopes that the buyer will be somehow impressed with their presentation, proposal or quote and want to move forward.

There are a number of ways sellers can qualify and extract commitments and obligations from buyers prior to giving a proposal or presentation. They can get the buyer to agree prior to giving a proposal that the buyer will agree to make a decision about what if anything the next step will be when the proposal or presentation is presented. Doing this requires the seller to have a very strong upfront conversation with the buyer about what'll happen at the time the presentation or proposal is presented. The seller must be willing to straighten their backbone and have the guts to extract a commitment for a decision prior to giving a presentation or proposal. Failing to do this will almost certainly guarantee a stall or put off when the presentation or proposal is made.

Another courageous but seldom used tactic that should be employed by the seller is to require that the buyer pay for the proposal upfront. In this scenario, the seller agrees to give a full-blown presentation and proposal and in return the buyer agrees to pay for the proposal. In this case the seller will take possession of the proposal and will be allowed to use the information contained in the proposal in any manner that he or she sees fit.

The seller gets paid for their efforts in making the proposal and the buyer gets a customized solution. This is a win-win for both parties and eliminates one party from extracting an unfair concession from the other. This requires skills, guts, a new belief system and abundant mentality on the part of the seller. An additional benefit to the seller is that it positions the seller as someone whose service is in great demand and minimizes or eliminates the perception that he is a beggar. Employing this strategy does not guarantee that the seller will make a sale. It does, however, increase the buyer's respect for the salesperson and the self image of the salesperson.

Another strategy to be used by the seller is to quit leaving written proposals with prospect or buyers who fail to make a commitment to move to the next that in the selling process. This involves having a very frank and open discussion with a potential buyer before a presentation or proposal is given and explaining to the buyer that contrary to how most companies operate that the sellers company policy is not to leave presentations and proposals that contain proprietary information. Adopting this policy will minimize or eliminate the ability of the buyer to use the seller's information to negotiate a better deal from a competitor. Again this requires guts, discipline and a change in beliefs that somehow potential buyers will balk at this approach.

....

How To Gain An Initial Commitment From The Prospect Before The Appointment

Salespeople have many erroneous beliefs. One of the most pervasive and damaging beliefs they have is that they should schedule appointment with every prospect or buyer that will agree to see them. It's this mistaken belief that causes them to run helter-skelter throughout their territory wasting hours and hours meeting with any and every potential buyer in hopes that their efforts will result in finding sufficient numbers of buyers who will do business with them.

The reality of this process is that less than half - considerably less - of the prospects that they have initial appointments with do not end up becoming clients. There is something terribly wrong with a process that fails 60% to 70% of the time. And even though salespeople admit to the high failure rate of this process, they continue to do the same behavior over and over and over again. They do so because they don't know any better and because they do not have a more effective process.

A more effective approach and process would require that the prospect earn the right to receive a visit from the salesperson. One of the ways of doing this is to have the prospect complete what we at New School Selling call an Uncovery Worksheet. This Uncovery Worksheet contains a series of questions that the prospect is asked to complete and fax or e-mail to the sales person prior to the first face to face to meeting.

Requiring the prospect to complete this worksheet prior to the first face-to-face meeting does two things: number one, it determines the prospects level of commitment and reveals their willingness to be open and truthful; secondly, it gives the salesperson some basic understanding of the problems, issues and concerns that the prospect has. Knowing these issues ahead of time the salesperson is able to ascertain whether it makes any sense or not for both parties to commit their time to meet with each other. In some cases the answers from the Uncovery Worksheet will disqualify the prospect as someone that the salesperson should meet with. If the prospect balks, resists or fails to complete the Uncovery Worksheet they have simply disqualified themselves as a serious prospect with which the salesperson should spend their time.

This unorthodox and nontraditional approach is often met with great resistance by sales people who, incorrectly, believe that this approach will lead to fewer closed sales. It will not. What it will do is reduce the number of first-time appointments and proposals that are generated by the sales team. The number of closed sales will remain the same or increase and closing percentages will skyrocket. The end result is fewer wasted appointments, fewer wasted proposals being generated, and more deals closed in less time.

CHAPTER 4: DEVELOPING TRUST AND RESPECT

Everything is a Commodity

According to Theodore Levitt, a Harvard Business School professor, "The purpose of a business is to find and keep customers and to get existing buyers to continue doing business with you rather than your competitors". I couldn't agree more.

In the old days of selling, the best way to get customers was to have the best products at the best prices. That is still important: but in a much more competitive world the benchmarks for products and price are rapidly being met by many of your competitors. Pick any industry and you will find products, services and prices all beginning to look alike and blur together. To the customer, even salespeople all tend to look alike. They ask the same questions, wear the same suits, write the same proposals and make the same promises. From the customer's point of view there isn't much differentiation out there.

Step back and look at the relationship between buyer and seller and how it has changed as the world has become more competitive. With more options that look alike, and are sold alike, buyers make decisions to go with one product or another on the basis of what perceived difference is left: price and convenience. Customers tend to buy the best price and most convenient arrangement from the options presented (I didn't say sold).

Because salespeople are not very good at differentiating themselves from the competition, buyers simply make a transactional buying decision instead of a decision based on relationship. In a transactional relationship the customer simply gets an order taker not a professional salesperson.

In the final analysis we have to realize that the traditional process of calling on customers and quoting price and pitching product is dead. It has been replaced by a new paradigm that sees professional salespeople as business partners or trusted advisors. If you want to survive and compete, quit pitching product and price and learn how to present yourself as a business partner or trusted advisor. Many companies and salespeople have yet to realize this. As a result, they will be left in the dust.

....

Stop Acting Like a Salesperson

To stop getting treated like a stereotypical salesperson stop acting like one.

How does a stereotypical salesperson act? They try to convince, persuade, and sometimes manipulate through the use of psychological tricks. No one likes to be treated that way. Think about it. How do you feel when someone tries to convince or persuade you?

Yet that is what sales trainers have taught sales people for the last fifty years. Before I started New School Selling, I spent sixteen years in the sales profession. I received hundreds of hours of sales training. And not one company I ever worked for really knew how to teach salespeople anything but persuasion and manipulation. Most of this training, we were told, was based on "solid psychological theory" and sound human "relationship principles". In reality it was psychological warfare. Us against them. It produced an adversarial relationship.

What else do stereotypical salespeople do to alienate prospects? They vomit on the prospect about the features and benefits of their product or service. They spend hours extolling the virtues of their product without knowing if the prospect has the slightest interest in what they are saying. They are taught this in product knowledge training. They are taught that if you just talk long enough you might hit the prospect's hot button.

What should you do? Stop trying to use psychological tricks and gimmicks with prospects. Start being blatantly honest with them. Stop promoting the company line about how great your products are and start talking to your prospects about what matters to them. Talk to them about what is important to them not to you. And quit trying to "pitch" everyone who can fog a mirror.

Prospects buy things for their reasons not yours. In fact, sometimes they buy in spite of your reasons. Most importantly, before you start talking about your product, establish some mutual trust and respect. People don't buy from people they like but they do buy from people they trust and respect. Spend time earning their trust and respect instead of trying to do battle with them.

....

Why People Judge You Instantly

Here is a powerful quote from Executive EQ, by Robert Cooper, Ph.D. on developing trust and respect. I think it gives us all food for thought.

"What few managers realize is that intuitions, emotional contact, influence, trust, believability are all processed in the preconscious areas of the brain -- in particular, the limbic system, which servers not only as a gateway to the sites where cognition, or thinking, takes place but as the brain's emotional center. Whereas the cognitive brain centers devote their time sifting through words, concepts, and analysis, the emotional brain continuously scans for meaning and judgment from thousands of subtle nuances in voice tone, gestures, eye contact, and a wide range of other behaviors that the cognitive brain centers scarcely register or understand. The limbic system works approximately 80,000 times faster than the conscious cerebral cortex. The conscious mind can process only 126 bits of information per second and only 40 bits of human speech, yet our senses can receive up to 100 million bits of input per second. The limbic gives us an instantaneous 'reading' on believability and trustworthiness during each of our interactions with others. In short: Without believability, we are neither heard or trusted."

All of this happens without conscious recognition. In business and social situations people are judging, rightly or wrongly, you instantly.

....

Why Do Prospects Resist Salespeople?

How do you react when someone tries to persuade you to do something you don't want to do? If you are normal, you almost always resist. If he or she continues trying to convince you that what they want you to do is good for you, how do you react? If you are normal, you resist even more.

If another person gives you all kinds of positive reasons to do what you don't what to do, and tells you that there are no reasons not to, what do you do? If you are normal, you'll find all kinds of reasons why you shouldn't do it. You figure that other person is hiding the truth - the whole picture - from you. You begin to feel that that person is not someone you can trust and you don't want to have anything to do with someone like that. That's the way most people react to that kind of treatment.

How does this apply to selling? Research shows that over eighty (80) percent of all people want to do business with a salesperson they can really trust and respect. Yet, almost all salespeople sell by attempting to persuade and convince prospects to buy something they don't want. And they do it in a way that causes them be perceived as someone who bends the truth (lies).

If you want dramatic improvements in your closing rates, you need to make radical changes in the way you sell.

Stop trying to convince people to do business with you.

Learn to be totally upfront with people by telling them what problems you solve and then ask them if they have any of those problems and if so do they want to fix them. If they don't have any of those problems or don't have the commitment to fix those problems politely end the conversation and move on.

Buying is an Emotional Decision

Buying is an emotional decision. People buy emotionally and then justify their decision intellectually. For proof of this look at the advertising business. Michelin Tire Company became the number one tire company in the world when they put that baby in the tire. People who buy Michelins are not buying four -ply vulcanized rubber. They are buying trust, safety and security all of which are emotions. Those are some of the same emotions people rely on when they buy anything.

Here are some statistics for you. All studies of human motivation conclude that people buy from people they trust and respect. As much as 50 to 80% of the reason people buy anything has to do with trust and respect. When people buy your product chances are that they don't fully comprehend the technical aspects of what you sell. What they do understand is that they feel comfortable, trust and respect the person they are talking with. The greatest skill any sales professional can develop is the ability to connect or bond with the prospect emotionally.

....

Watch Your Tonality

According to the science of neurolinguistic programming, as much as 83% of the communicated message on the phone is the use of tonality. Tonality has to do with rate of speech, volume, pacing, pitch, and rhythm. The goal of tonality is to mirror and match (not imitate) the person you are speaking with. For example, if you are speaking with someone who is talking a bit slower than you adjust your pace to reflect his or her pace. The voice is a tool to a salesperson just as a wrench is to a mechanic. Learn to use this valuable tool. I have used a voice coach to both video and audio tape my phone calls and my classroom training. It was amazing to both listen to and watch myself. I would urge you to get a tape recorder and begin to record and debrief your phone calls.

....

Emotion vs Logic

When people buy an ice cream cone, they don't buy a lump of fat and sugar. To the ice cream lover, a delicious cone is a spirit lifter, stress buster or hunger reliever.

When your prospect buys your product or service what emotion are they buying? While you may be providing perfectly practical benefits, selling features and benefits is purely intellectual. Most customers are motivated more by the emotional benefits they get from what you sell rather than logical benefits. People buy emotionally and then justify logically.

For example, people don't normally buy a car strictly because it is a good way to get across town. Instead they purchase the thrill of speed, the prestige of getting admiring looks, or the confidence of safety.

Recently, I got a book from Amazon.com. It came packaged with a free bookmark. On it was a quote, "When you sell a man a book, you don't sell him twelve ounces of paper, ink and glue – you sell him a whole new life."

Make sure your sales and marketing efforts shout the dream you provide. Learn to appeal to the emotional nature of your prospect's humanness.

What Are Buyers Afraid Of

We live in a world full of uncertainty, fear and anxiety. Stock market crashes, terrorists attacks and wars are all part of our daily lives. Our fear and anxiety is constantly being nurtured and reinforced by every print and electronic media we encounter. Tragedy is brought to us in real time "live" and "up close and personal". Information that used to take hours or days to reach us now reaches us in real time. We have become what some futurists are calling victims of "psychic distress."

Nowhere is this more evident than in the world of marketing and selling.

Because buyers have been bombarded with so much hype, over promotion and razzle -dazzle they have become jaded, skeptical and cynical of everything they hear and see.

They take nothing at face value. Their belief is that a marketer is guilty until proven innocent. They believe that anything that you tell a sales-person can and will be used against you. As a result, they hesitate to share any information or reveal anything of substance about their situation. **You can't really blame them can you?**

What are some of the most common fears buyers have about the selling process:

1. Fear of making a mistake

Buyers are afraid that even though buying from you today looks like the thing to do, they'll regret that decision tomorrow, next week, or next month. They fear buying something that they don't really need or paying more than they should. The higher the price and the more choices they have to pick from the greater the fear.

2. Fear of losing respect of self and others

Many people have a need for the social approval of others. They are afraid that someone: a spouse, friend, peer, co-worker or a boss will say something like, "I can't believe you bought that" or I can't believe you paid that much for that".

Some buyers fear that the wrong decision might mean a loss of promotion, or prestige. Worse they fear it could result in termination. As a result, they delay and drag out the process hoping that they won't make a mistake.

3. Fear of the unknown.

Regardless of assurances and guarantees from you, buyers may be more content to stick with a painful status quo than to opt for an uncertain future. They may not like what they currently have but the future is too big a question mark to take any risks. This fear is especially pronounced for buyers whose job may not be assured or for those who lack self-confidence.

4. Fear of losing control

Like all people, buyers want to feel that they have choices and are in control. They want to establish the agenda and control the timing. They are comforted by being able to delay purchase decisions as long as they can. Once they feel that they are losing that control their fears skyrocket.

Some these anxieties are obvious; others are subtle. You'll increase your influence and credibility once you help your buyers discover and confront their fears, show that you are sensitive to those fears, and help them come to discover that your product or service will eliminate their fear and provide them with peace of mind.

....

When You Think You Are In Heaven And Find Out You Are In Hell

Recently, I had two clients call to say that they lost their number one account. In one case it cost the agent $80,000 in lost commissions and in the other the loss was over $50,000. In both cases these agents had maintained these accounts for several years. So what happened?

We could speculate as to why these agents lost this business, but we will never really be sure. However, both cases share some common threads. Both accounts originally started with the agent dealing one on one with the owner. As time passed and the businesses grew, the owners became less involved in the insurance decisions and delegated those decisions to a staff member. The agent was essentially handed off to someone with whom they had little or no relationship.

As each of these agents related their side of the story to me, it became apparent that the agent had mistakenly assumed that they no longer needed to nurture, strengthen and grow the relationships within the company. They essentially had taken the existing relationship

for granted and had failed to realize that they needed to continue to "court and woo" their client. It is the same mistake that marriage partners make when they begin to take their spouse for granted.

A parable explains this well. A man who was dying was presented with the option of visiting both heaven and hell to see where he would like to spend eternity.

When he visited heaven he observed a very serene and peaceful atmosphere. The streets were paved with gold and angels floated through the air playing harps and cellos. People munched on nectar and fruit and were friendly, though somewhat sedated and tranquil. Not a bad place at all.

When he visited hell he was shocked. Instead of fire and brimstone there were people dancing and partying and drinking. There was a great variety and abundance of sumptuous and delectable foods. People were laughing and telling jokes and it reminded him of his college fraternity days.

When it came time to choose, he chose hell. You can't really blame him can you?

When he died and got there it was horrible. People were wailing and screaming. It was miserably hot and not a drop of water to be had. The only food available was scraps that people fought over viciously.

Unable to comprehend what had happened he asked his host, "When I took the tour there were people dancing and partying and drinking. There was a great variety abundance of sumptuous and delectable foods. People were laughing and telling jokes. What happened?" With a grin on his face and a gleam in his eye his host responded and said, "before you were a prospect now you are a client."

The moral: The way you keep clients is to treat them, after they become a customer, the same as you did before they became a customer.

CHAPTER 5: PAIN

....

What Really Motivates
Prospects to Buy

Overview of Pain

This section will teach you how to ask the right questions at the beginning and throughout the sales process so you will not be plagued with put-offs, delays, and indecisiveness from the prospect. What would your sales results be if you could get decisions from your prospects at then end of each step of your sales process? How much time are you wasting now on prospects that will never buy? You are going to learn the real reasons why prospects are motivated to buy and how to ask the right questions to get your prospect to "open up" and tell you their reasons. Let's get started.

Look at these words and read then either out load or to yourself:

> Assistance
> Asset
> Comfort
> Convenience

Improvement

Return

Superiority

Faster

Better

Lower cost

Now read these words either out loud or to yourself:

Discomfort

Distress

Irritation

Strain

Trouble

Problems

Which group of words do you think would motivate a prospect to take immediate action? Would they be more likely to take action if they had an immediate **problem** or some type of **distress** or discomfort? Or, would they be more motivated to take immediate action if they had the opportunity to **improve** or increase the **convenience** of something, or that something become **better**, *faster* or more efficient?

If you answered these questions like most business decision makers do, then you would have said that the "troublesome" words are more likely to cause prospects take immediate action.

Immediate action, or "decision making" is what makes a sale "close" or become a sale. If your prospect cannot or will not make a decision of some sort, (even if their decision is "no") then all you end up with is a delay. The fact is that most "delays" end up becoming a "no", but most salespeople are uncomfortable asking the right questions to get the prospect to give them a decision.

Let's work on understanding what really motivates your prospects to take action and let's learn how to ask the right questions to make this happen.

If you can cause your prospect to talk about his problems and openly discuss the ramifications of not taking prompt action to correct this problem, then you will have caused your prospect to "feel" the pain of his problem, and that is what motivates the prospect to take action and make a buying decision.

A Common Tale

Here's a short story to illustrate this point.

Robert was a typical energetic salesperson in his late thirties, who was successful with his company. He had been promoted up the ranks almost each year and now was in a key position within his organization. Over the past several months, Robert had been working particularly hard to ensure he would get the next promotion. Now that he had accomplished that goal, he decided it was time to get back in optimal physical condition.

He stopped in to visit a health club he wanted to join, picked up a beautiful color brochure, and took it home to his wife to share his enthusiasm. After a quick hello and kiss on the cheek he took the brochure out of his suit pocket and said, "Honey, this is just what I need. I've been working so hard to get the promotion. I've been feeling a little tired and I know that I have not been taking good care of myself and this would be a great benefit for me. Look at these pictures and how beautiful this club is." His wife Susan smiled and looked on. Robert continued enthusiastically, "They have all the newest equipment and within a few months, I'll be looking like I did when I was in my twenties." Susan said "this looks nice, how much does this cost?" "That's the best part" said Robert, "It's only one seventy-five a month and you and the kids can come anytime for just ten dollars each per visit. Susan's expression change quickly. "One seventy five a month… That's… um … over two thousand dollars a year! Have you considered just getting on an exercise program at home like bike riding or running? Wouldn't that do the same thing?" "Susan, this has all of the best machines and all of the best facilities, I could be in such good shape" replied Robert. Susan spoke up, "Yes, but, we just can't spend two thousand dollars on a health club, we need that money so we can save for the addition to the house… And what about that cruise we talked about for our tenth anniversary, isn't that more important than a fancy health club when you can do the same thing here at home?" Robert thought about it quickly and decided to drop the subject altogether. He saw he was getting nowhere.

Now, Fast forward 30 days….

It's about two o'clock one humid afternoon when Susan gets a call. "Hello, honey, It's me, Robert." Sue immediately said, "Rob What's wrong, you don't sound like yourself". I'm fine, it's just that I'm in the hospital, but there's nothing to worry about. I'm OK, I just passed out at work, and they took me here, but I'm OK.

Susan made a bee line for the hospital where she raced to his side. The doctor had just come in to talk to Robert. "You must be Susan", the doctor said, "Robert kept telling me about you when we were working on him. Let me tell you both what happened. Rob, you had a very mild episode, probably just due to stress and lack of exercise, but it could have been worse. You don't seem to be getting much physical activity and your weight is going to cause more problems if you can't lose about 20 pounds. I'd suggest a routine physical activity program and that you cut your fat intake and eat smaller portions…if you don't want this to happen again. I'll discharge you today, but I suggest you get back in shape."

Susan looked at Rob with concerned eyes, "That's it" she said sharply. "You're joining that health club next week". Rob looked puzzled and said cautiously, "but that's so expensive, and we have other priorities like the house and the cru..… Susan cut him off before he could finish his sentence. " I don't care about those things, you're joining the health club and I don't care about what it costs. Now, if you don't mind, we're picking up the phone right now and were going to get this done today, here's my credit card…give me the phone book right now.

So why did Susan's perspective change so quickly? Thirty days earlier Susan perceived Rob's joining the health club as an "improvement" or a "better way" or a "benefit" But now, because she had experienced **Discomfort, Distress, and "potential" Trouble and Problems,** money did not matter and she insisted on immediate action.

You will learn how to ask the right questions to cause your prospects to talk about their problems and their trouble. Can you see why bombarding your prospect with features and benefits, beautiful brochures, and "reasons to buy" are ineffective, compared to causing them to talk about their problems and troubles? There is nothing wrong with great marketing materials, but that will not cause the prospect to **_feel_** their pain, trouble, and problems.

The Problem Identification Process (PIP)

The "PIP" is a series of questions and statements which will help you and your prospect focus on the impact of their problems, troubles, aches, & pains. It moves the prospect from the general to the specific and from the intellectual to the emotional.

PIP Diagram

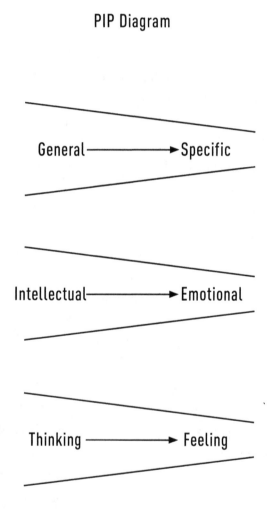

General ——————► Specific

Intellectual ——————► Emotional

Thinking ——————► Feeling

Pain

Most of the people who are in need of what you sell don't even know they have a need. If you are to be successful, you must identify your target market and begin to contact those people. It helps if you have a mega advertising and marketing budget, and deep enough pockets to wait for a branding campaign to work.

If you don't have these financial resources, another way to do this is to pick up the phone and call these people to see if they have any interest in talking with someone who does what you do. This approach is not complicated or difficult.

If you are tempted to discount the effectiveness of this approach because you dislike calling strangers, you may want to reconsider, because I have taught this concept to thousands of sales people who have used it effectively. The key to its effectiveness is having the discipline to consistently execute the activity.

Here is an example:

"Hi John, this is Steve Clark. May I take 30 seconds and tell you why I called?"

Most people will say OK. Some will not. Don't worry about it. Just hang up and call someone else. This unusual opening surprises Broca and causes them to think about what you just asked.. Once they give you permission to continue you say,

"I work with Business Owners who want to:

Recruit and hire better quality sales people,

Implement a more effective accountability process,

Shorten their sales cycle or

Eliminate discounting in competitive situations

Pause for a couple of seconds to let what you just said sink in. Then continue with, "John, may I ask you a question?"

When you receive permission you say,

"Are any of these things important enough for you to spend two minutes talking about?"

If they say yes continue by asking "Which of these issues is the most important?"

Engage them in dialogue and continue to ask questions to help them discover for themselves if they need what you have.

With practice you can make 35 dials per hour, contact 5 to 7 people, and make one appointment. If you do this one hour daily Monday thru Friday for 50 weeks you should be able to set 250 new appointments in a year.

What would that do for your business?

....

Pain vs Gain

Which is a better motivator of human behavior - fear of loss or anticipation of gain? For the definitive answer we need to look no further than Professors Daniel Kahneman, who was awarded the 2002 Noble Prize in economic sciences, and Amos Tversky who originally described "Prospect Theory" in 1979.

They found that people placed different weights on gains and losses and that individuals are much more distressed by prospective losses than they are excited by equivalent gains. Some economists have concluded that investors typically consider the loss of $1 dollar twice as painful as the pleasure received from a $1 gain.

In selling, we have known for some time that it is easier to sell someone who is currently experiencing psychological loss or "pain" than it is to sell someone who is not. Unfortunately, most salespeople don't recognize this and as a result they waste a lot of time attempting to convince, persuade or "close" someone who is not in "pain" by giving million dollar presentations in hopes that prospects will be blown away by the scintillating benefits of the product or service.

The truly successful salespeople know this bit of human motivation and spend their time culling through suspects until they find someone who is in "pain" and is committed to getting rid of that "pain".

> If you want to excel in selling become focused on finding "pain". No pain no sale.

You can take that to the bank.

....

Selling Is A "Whole – Brainer"

Psychologist Roger Sperry received the Nobel prize in 1981 for his discovery that the human brain has specialized functions on the right and left side. He found that the left hemisphere is the logical, rational, conscious side and that the right hemisphere is the emotional, intuitive unconscious side.

His discovery has powerful applications in the fields of sales, marketing and advertising. While we have known, intuitively – a right side view- for some time that most people buy emotionally and justify logically, we really never knew why or how until Sperry made his discovery.

That people make buying decisions emotionally or unconsciously is further validated by Joseph LeDoux, Ph.D, a world-renowned neuroscientist at New York University in an interview with the Gallup Management Journal in December of 2003.

In response to the question, "how much does the unconscious influence things like purchase decisions?", LeDoux responds, "In truth, most of what we do, we do unconsciously, and then rationalize the decision consciously after the fact".

If you want to have influence as a marketer or sales person it is imperative that you learn how to appeal to the right brain. To do this you must quit trying to sell using a left brain logical, rational approach that focuses on products, features and benefits and start connecting with people on the emotional, intuitive, unconscious level.

Getting the prospect to talk about his problems

As you might imagine, it takes some knowledge and some practice to become skilled at getting the prospect to open up about his problems.

One way to think about this process is to imagine yourself as a skilled physician. A skilled physician begins by asking general questions; questions about what's bothering you, and then as you answer those questions he gets more and more specific.

He doesn't start off by poking you where it hurts the most. That poking might identify the problem but it certainly doesn't feel very good to you and you will not feel very good about coming back to this doctor. We, as salespeople, can use the same technique as the skilled physician.

Here's how to accomplish this same process in sales.

Asking Broad Questions

Process overview (BSD):

Ask **B**road questions

Get more **S**pecific about each problem

"**D**rill down" on each of the specific problems

Begin by asking some **B**road questions. Here are some examples of broad questions.

Broad Questions

Is there anything about your present situation you don't like?

What do you like about what you are currently using?

What would you like to change or improve if anything?

Isn't what you already have doing the job?

In your industry we've noticed a problem with….have you experienced any problems in this area?

Do you have any problems in relation to….

Where do you see a need for improvement?

When did you first decide you should look into….?

How do you see me helping out?

Why did you agree to see me?

Specific Questions

How do you see that working for you?

How long has this been a problem?

If you were to change, what would you do differently?

If you were to pick one thing that you didn't like about that, what would it be?

What if the Prospect Won't Admit They Have any Problems

It's not unusual for prospects to want to hide their cards from you. After all, they may perceive you as a typical salesperson and in their eyes, you are trying to manipulate and trick then into buying something they don't want. Therefore, they withhold and withdraw. It's not that they are bad people; it's just that they are trying to protect their interest.

Here are some questions to ask the prospect if you are not making any progress using the initial questions. Be aware that it is imperative that you ask these questions in a **genuine and nurturing manner.** You do not want to be perceived as facetious or flippant. Be genuine when you ask these questions. They are direct and to the point.

Does that mean that you're not open to new ideas?

I want to ask you a question, but I feel if I ask you, you're going to get upset.

How do I tell you you're making the wrong decision without you getting upset?

What are you thinking about?

Why did you invite me over?

CHAPTER 6: SALES MANAGEMENT

Why Sales Training Doesn't Usually Work

In 1988, according to the American Society for Training and Development, only 19% of people who took a training course received any kind of sustained performance improvement. There have been numerous articles in many publications which confirm that premise. Why?

According to Herb Greenberg, co-author of the book *"How To Hire and Develop Your Next Top Performer"* there is a very logical reason that only 19% of sales training participants benefit from sales training. Greenberg, who is the co-developer of the Caliper Profile, says that 55% of people who are in sales do not possess the necessary psychological or emotional skills to ever be successful. These people should do themselves, their employer and their prospects a favor by getting out of the profession.

Another 25% of salespeople are in sales environments that are not suited to their personal strengths (i.e., they are suited for inside sales but they are in outside sales or vice versa or they sell a tangible item but really are better suited to sell an intangible, etc.). These people could be successful if they were matched to the right sales environment. That only leaves 20% of the people who are in sales actually doing what they are naturally suited to do. The reason that only 20% of people who attend sales training receive any significant, long-term benefit is that they are the only ones who should be there to begin with. Not everyone is trainable.

Companies waste millions of dollars each year sending people to sales training. Many of these people don't want to be there, will not benefit from being there and should really be doing something else with their time.

When salespeople under perform, training is not always the magic cure. So, instead of hiring warm bodies and then trying to train them, companies would do well to concentrate their resources on developing better hiring and recruiting practices. This would result in hiring stronger salespeople who could benefit from training.

There is an old southern expression that says it best:

"You can't make a silk purse out of a sow's ear."

How true that is.

Coaching to Win

What's the one thing that every manager wants more of? The typical answer is resources or revenue – real answer is time. Today the typical manager's agenda is packed to the breaking point not just with such activities as market planning, budgeting, and recruiting, but with increasing loads of what this harried professional calls "administrivia".

Volumes have been written about how to manage your time more effectively. The best advice I can offer is this: Give priority to tasks that get the best performance out of your people. That means put coaching employees at the top of your to-do list.

The manager whose first priority is developing his people knows that frequent coaching delivers consistent financial results. Regular scheduling of coaching and review must be an agenda item that's written in ink, not penciled in.

Coaching is a system that "grows" people by enabling them to learn through guided discovery, not by showing or telling people what to do. Telling is not coaching! Coaching assumes that team members learn by doing. Effective coaches have three major responsibilities:

1. Guiding people to discover the tools they need to get the job done.

2. Building confidence.

3. Motivating team members to be the best they can be.

....

How to Coach Like a Pro

Here are the seven stages that identify the coaching process:

1. **Mutual Agreement** You and your team member agree on the specific project that he or she will be responsible for. This project represents something that would enhance your team member's competence and once mastered by your team member, take a load off your shoulders.

2. **Avoid misunderstandings** by identifying the goals and outcomes expected. So often things don't go the way you expect because your team member doesn't understand the outcomes you want to achieve in the first place. Both of you should be very clear about the when, where, what, who and how. Always set high expectations and provide accountability. In the long run, you get the type and quality of performance you expect and accept.

3. **Facilitate self-discovery** This requires you to talk less, listen more. Listen twice as much as you talk. Your role is to facilitate the thinking of your team members, not think for them! If a team member comes to you and asks you to make a decision, ask him or her: "What do you think?"

4. **Agree on the boundaries** Identify your mission, vision, and core values, as these represent mutually accepted parameters and boundaries. You may need to supplement them so that team members know where your comfort zone is and where the danger zone begins.

5. **Authorize and empower** To get the job done team members need authorization, including the appropriate spending authority to get the job done. Tell your team members how far they can go without coming to you, and then stay out of their way and let them do their thing.

6. **Summarize and reality test** If the project is critical do some reality testing by having the team member state in his or her own words what, specifically, the two of you have agreed to. "Please summarize for me what you are going to do between now and the next time we meet."

7. **Track and follow through** Put a note on your calendar or computerized tickler file that will remind you of the date and time your team member promised to provide you with a report, update, or feedback. Then stand back and don't interfere! Now, watch your team member grow, and watch the dramatic improvements in performance, productivity, and profitability.

Think of coaching and developing a team as the equivalent of exercise. You know it's good for you, and you know it gets results. But in a high-stress marketplace, you also know that you could easily shove the coaching aside every time something more pressing comes up, just like you blow off going to the gym when you have to work late. With your in-box overflowing and six calls to return, it's easy to say: "Can't we postpone this to a more convenient time?"

There's no magic pill that will force you to institute regular coaching. But here's one big reason to take it very seriously: The better the practice, the better the performance. Coaching will always be the best way to spend your time.

....

What Makes a Great Sales Force?

Many of the world's best sales forces are the best because they have developed and used a systematic sales process. Having a map of the things we salespeople have to do to make a sale provides a framework for sales planning and activity that reduces mistakes and shortens hew hire ramp-up time. However, what is conspicuously absent from most of these process maps are the things that our prospective customers have to do each step of the way in order to buy. The truth is that the things we do at any particular step or stage in the process could be a complete waste of time if the client doesn't do what they must do to move forward to the next step or stage in the buying process.

As sales professionals, you and I don't retire quota or earn commissions for anything that we do. We get paid on what our prospects do. When they sign a contract or issue a purchase order, then we make some money. This is the root of one of the major challenges of selling. We have to accept that we cannot control our prospects.

As salespeople or managers we often ask, "What do we have to do to close this deal?" That, in fact, is the wrong questions. What we should be asking is, "What does the prospect have to do in order to buy?" and then the follow-on questions is, "What do we have to do to get them to do those things?"

Whether or not we have or follow a systematic sales process, we should endeavor to understand and document our client's buying process. We must understand not only the things that have to happen throughout the selection and approval process, but who will be involved along the way.

Armed with a thorough understanding of the steps and stages of our prospects buying process, we can plan our work accordingly. Then every single move we make can be made with the specific intent of enabling or empowering our prospect to take the next step they need to take in order to buy.

If you think about it for a minute, before we speak to a prospective prospect on the phone we should know and understand exactly what has to happen next in their buying process, and what we're going to do on this call to make that happen. And if we spend the time and money to go visit a prospect without a plan of what we intend to say and do to help them take the next step in the buying process, then we are little more than a professional visitor.

Defining and documenting a useful map of our prospects buying process will take time, it will take effort, and it will require that we reach, qualify, and sell to all of the people who will play a part in the selection and approval process. We will need a lot of input and per-spective because simply accepting only one person's opinion of their process leaves too many variables to chance and ultimately leaves us with too much exposure and opportunity for failure. Taking the time to thoroughly understand all of the things that the prospect needs to do in order to buy often makes the difference between the very successful and those who simply get by.

....

Effective Sales Management

The job of a sales manager is not to grow sales but to **recruit, grow and develop** salespeople.

The sales manager's job is to set the course and direction of the sales team by developing and implementing the most efficient system of selling the company's products and services. By his/her statements and actions, the successful sales manager **inspires and motivates** the sales team to act in ways that promote everyone's best interest.

The sales manager's role is to cultivate and refine the talents of the salespeople and he/she should make sure that the salespeople are aware of this. It is important that the effective sales manager communicate the purpose behind their efforts to help the salespeople grow their skills. When done properly the successful sales manager is able to institute a culture of "excellence" as the prime motivator for increasing sales performance.

The Four Components of Effective Sales Management

An effective sales management process contains four components.

Recruiting, Developing Accountability, Coaching, and Motivating.

Let's take a look at each of these:

Recruiting

Sales is a career with enormous opportunity. For those who are ambitious, sales is an extremely attractive profession. A sales career offers high income, personal freedom, and limitless opportunities.

With all of these benefits why is it so hard for companies to attract, recruit, build and maintain a highly productive sales team? With all that the sales profession offers it should be easy to attract and hire the best and brightest talent. Why then do most companies experience high turnover, complacency, mediocre production and poor attitudes with their sales teams?

The reason that companies experience these things is that 4 out of 5 people now should be doing something else for themselves, for their company, for the profession and certainly for the sake of the prospects they encounter. Because these people do not have the natural talent, they try to fake it and in the fast talking process, sell themselves and the rest of us short. Of the 80% of people now selling – 55% of them should be in another profession because they have neither the emotional or psychological talents to succeed in selling.

Another 25% who are selling are miscast. That is they are selling the wrong product or service. They are trying to sell a product for which they are not suited, i.e., they are an outside sales person when they would be better suited to be an inside salesperson. Or they are selling an intangible when they would be better suited to sell a tangible product, etc.

So how do companies find themselves in this situation? It can all be traced back to ineffective recruiting practices and processes. Let's take a look at the typical recruiting practices of companies.

Typical recruiting practices usually fall into one of two categories: the traditional approach or the warm body approach.

In the traditional approach companies emphasize such selection criteria as: previous experience, age, race, sex or education although none of these have been validated as any predictable indicator of success in selling.

In the warm body approach companies will hire most anybody and pay them little or no salary, promise them high commissions, provide little or no training and put them on the street. It's the "throw a lot of mud on the wall" and see what sticks approach.

Using either of these two approaches is sure to produce mediocrity at best. At worst, because incompetent people are put on the street, it educates prospects that salespeople are unprofessional, ill-trained, high pressure, con artists. It is also the reason that the sales profession is the butt of many jokes.

So what's the solution to this problem?

Companies must change their thinking. They need to view recruiting as a process, not an event. It should be an on going and continuous. Recruiting to the sales manager is what prospecting is to a salesperson. Just as a salesperson should have a pipeline of qualified prospects, so should the manager have a "bank of people" he/she can engage in the recruiting process.

Here are some steps a manager can take to keep the recruiting pipeline filled:

- **Develop a sales profile of the position you are looking to fill.** Determine what percentage of the job requires opening new accounts versus servicing existing clients. How long is the sales cycle of your produce or service. Will the salesperson do the prospecting or will they be provided with leads. Who will they call on. How much technical background do they need. Will they sell a customer and move on or is it sell and customer development. How much sales management pressure will they receive. What is the compensation plan. What skill sets do they need. What is the emotional and psychological profile for a successful hire. Once these things are outlined it is a matter of recruiting someone who matches up to at least 80% of the Profile. The bottom line to sales success is job match. Sales winners win because they are doing what they are naturally programmed to do. Sales losers lose because they are trying to perform in a role that they are not naturally programmed for. No amount of coaching, training or mentoring can change someone's natural programming. The hiring decision is the most important decision a sales manager will ever make.

- **Set a goal to interview a specific number of people a month** (even if you don't intend to hire). This ensures that you always have a fresh group of people to talk with. This "practice" will help keep your interviewing skills sharp.

- **Advertise on a consistent, regular basis.** The helps to keep the pipeline full.

- **Offer recruiting bonuses and incentives to your salespeople.** After all, they know what the job entails.

- **Use Pre-Hire Assessments** to identify the emotional and psychological makeup of a potential new hire.

- **Develop more effective interviewing skills.** Since most sales managers don't interview regularly, they don't keep their skills sharp. Interviewing, like any other skill, requires constant practice to stay sharp.

Accountability

Unfortunately, we live in a modern culture that does not emphasize personal responsibility. The result is an epidemic of excuse making.

It is not my fault is the prevailing attitude of the masses. The sales manager is charged with the responsibility of **setting proper expectations**, developing systems to **track** and record sales activities and results and **eliminating any excuse making** when results are not achieved. Some of the sales activities that should be tracked and monitored **weekly** include:

- **Dials.** How many calls is the salesperson required to make daily?

- **Conversations.** How many dials does it take to reach a key decision maker?

- **Appointments Scheduled.** How many conversations does it take to schedule an appointment with a decision maker?

- **Appointments Kept.** How many scheduled appointments are kept.

- **Proposals.** How many first time appointments result in a proposal?

- **Sales.** How many proposals result in a sale? What is the revenue per sale?

The goal for the salespeople is to reach a point where they know what each call, conversation, appointment, proposal and sale is worth. When a salesperson knows this they can accurately forecast their current situation and set realistic future goals.

Knowing this information the manager can explain to the potential new hires exactly what is required and expected of them. This can be addressed during the pre-hire period and the sales candidate will know in advance what is required to succeed.

A salesperson cannot perform without knowing what is expected of them. Expectations spell out what is required to succeed, and it's best to explain this to the new hire during the training process.

For the more seasoned salespeople, other expectations might include:

- Number of new customers

- Dollars of revenue per period

- Gross profit margins

- Retention rate of existing customers

Coaching

The manager whose first priority is developing his people knows that frequent coaching delivers consistent financial results. Regular scheduling of coaching and review must be an agenda item that's written in ink, not penciled in.

Coaching is a system that "grows" people by enabling them to learn through **guided discovery**, not by showing or telling people what to do. Telling is not coaching! Coaching assumes that team members learn by doing. Effective coaches have three major responsibilities: (1) guiding people to discover the tools they need to get the job done; (2) building confidence; and (3) motivating team members to be the best they can be.

An effective sales manager juggles many balls in fulfilling his responsibility to the company, but none is more important than getting out in the field with their sales team. Too many sales managers are too busy shuffling papers, filling out reports and sitting behind their desks. They should be out making sales calls with their salespeople, helping to train them in more productive sales techniques.

There are three parts to coaching. They are **field coaching, pre and post call debriefing** and **coaching for improved performance.**

Field coaching has three parts: joint sales calls with the manager, training calls in which the salesperson observes the manager sell and coaching calls in which the manager observes.

- **Joint sales call** – working as a team the salesperson and the manager participate in the call equally. These double up calls not only increase sales but are also great learning experiences for the salesperson.

- **Training call** – the sales manager runs the call while the salesperson silently observes. It is important that the manager models the proper selling skills for the salesperson.

- **Coaching call** – the salesperson runs the call and the sales manager silently observes. At the end of the call the sales manager debriefs the salesperson and discusses lessons learned.

Coaching The Poor Peformer: To help a poor performer the coaching process would include these five steps:

- **Define the situation clearly** – gather facts and identify performance results.

- **Counsel** – meet with the rep and make it clear that your goal is to help them improve their performance. Avoid blaming, reprimanding or delivering ultimatums. Let the rep know that you believe that with coaching the performance issues can be improved.

- **Ask the salesperson** – what do you think the solution to the problem is. Solicit input from them on what they think they need to change. Avoid giving advice or telling the salesperson what they need to do.

- **Design a mutually agreed to plan** – this plan should be a comprehensive, clearly defined, results-oriented plan. The plan should include activity goals and results or production goals that both parties can agree to.

- **Set a follow-up** – following agreement on the plan, the rep must understand that the sales manager will closely scrutinize sales activity and results. The follow-up plan includes weekly meeting with the manager to go over results and progress.

When salespeople don't hit the targets, the manager needs to hold their feet to the fire. In some cases it may be necessary to renegotiate the expectations. But if the expectations were fair to begin with it is better for the manager to send the salesperson on to another career opportunity.

Motivating

A sales manager can motivate and inspire salespeople in three ways. Proper compensation plans, conducting effective sales and training meetings, and helping salespeople set higher goals and objectives.

Salespeople are motivated by ambition, the need for recognition, and of course compensation. To prompt salespeople to higher levels of performance it is necessary to design an effective compensation plan. An effective compensation plan is one that is going to help both the salesperson and the company achieve their goals.

Companies must incentivize the behavior and results they want. The comp plan should emphasize the desired company outcome. Be it new clients, retention of clients, new product sales or gross profits. Whatever the compensation plan is it needs to be easily understood by the salesperson. It should be so easily understood that the salesperson could figure it out in their head.

Sales meetings provide an excellent opportunity for motivating, training and inspiring salespeople. Unfortunately, most sales meetings fall short on this. Many times the sales meeting becomes a forum for the manager to rant and rave about lagging sales, lack of activity or administrative policies and details. Because of the social nature of most salespeople, sales meetings should be fun, educational and inspirational. It is also a place to publicly praise the sales team for *anything positive.* Salespeople get beat up constantly so use this time to *accentuate the positive and minimize the negative.* The salespeople should leave the sales meeting high as a kite not as low as a snake's belly. Most managers fail miserably in this role.

Training prepares the salesperson to maximize every customer encounter. A methodical selling process incorporates specific selling techniques that are custom-tailored for each buyer they interact with.

Through proper training, salespeople better understand their customer's wants and needs. They're also better equipped to cope with potential difficulties with the company's products and services.

Well-trained salespeople recognize genuine selling opportunities more readily than their untrained counterparts.

An effective training program brings new staff up to speed more quickly than when sales reps are forced to learn on their own. As a result, frustrations are minimized and people are less inclined to go elsewhere.

The third part of motivation is goal setting. The manager's role is to help salespeople become more focused on specific, achievable personal goals that are aligned with the company's goals. This requires spending time one-on-one with the salespeople to help them enlarge the mental picture they have of themselves and what they can achieve. Some examples of goals might include: sales and gross profits for the year, obtaining more business from existing clients, acquiring new clients, retention of existing clients, etc.

High performance starts with clear unambiguous goals. They must define what success means to the individual and to the company.

Sixteen Areas That Sales Training Will Improve

Is sales training an expense or an investment? The answer depends on and how effective the training is. Competent professional sales consulting will help companies improve in all of the following areas:

1. **More effective management of complex, big dollar deals:** Sales training can help you win the big ones by gaining a better understanding of the politics of larger organizations. Learn how to successfully navigate situations involving multiple decision makers, multiple departments, outside consultants, committees and unexpected participants.

2. **A shorter selling cycle:** Develop strong mutual agreements with prospective clients early in the selling cycle that define a step-by-step plan that will bring the process to an outcome within a mutually acceptable time frame.

3. **Higher comfort level calling at the "C" level:** Develop a selling readiness tool kit that quickly helps you establish credibility at the highest levels. Truly understanding your prospective client, their challenges and their vision is far more powerful than demonstrating your product knowledge or its wizardry.

4. **Weeding our non-buyers earlier:** Your time and your company's resources are extraordinarily valuable! Your prospect must earn them. Learn how to get prospects to sell you on their need and commitment.

5. **More effective prospecting:** Utilize a fresh, non-traditional approach to capture your prospect's interest and imagination on the first call. Then, quickly help them discover why it is in their best interest to invite you in.

6. **Less discounting:** Price is never the real issue! You will gain the confidence and skill to shift the buyer's focus from the price of your solution to: (a) the cost of not implementing your solution, and (b) their return on investment. If your customer really has the conviction that they'll get a significantly better return per invested dollar by going with you, they'll be glad to pay more!

7. **Higher per sale average:** Your will gain the confidence, patience and control required to do a thorough needs analysis before proposing any solution. This honest, comprehensive approach maximizes each opportunity by ensuring no money is left on the table, and that customers are totally satisfied.

8. **Better relationships with prospects and clients:** Create a climate of trust and respect through the utilization of a system where every conversation differentiates you from the stereotypical, ego-centered, pushy sales person. Experience the satisfaction of having your clients say, "Not only does he/she listen to me, they truly understand me."

9. **Higher closing ratios in competitive situations:** Through your superior knowledge of your prospect's needs and the precise execution of mutual agreements you will differentiate your solution, and yourself, from your competition.

10. **Lower cost per sale:** Precious resources previously wasted on non-buyers in unwarranted proposals, demos, on-sites, trials, and prototypes are now more productively allocated.

11. **More effective negotiations:** Bring about successful outcomes while making no unilateral concessions. Never give anything away unless you're getting something comparable, or of greater value in return.

12. **More effective team selling:** Experience the power of a selling team where every member is 100% bought-in to the exact same selling model. Every member always knows where they are in the process and what their exact role is.

13. **More accurate forecasting:** By achieving meaningful milestones throughout the selling cycle, the projected probability of a deal coming to fruition is within a significantly smaller margin of error. In addition, mechanisms are installed to protect the integrity of the overall forecasting system.

14. **Higher activity level per rep:** "The greatest motivator for a selling professional is winning", says Tom Peters, author of, In Search of Excellence. Fresh new tactics and strategies that really work deliver the kind of wins and successes that create a ground swell of excitement and activity.

15. Better internal communication: The consensus gained through effective implementation of an integrated, company-wide selling system and the common language to describe it, ensures every internal conversation between members of the team - managers, reps, sales engineers, consultants, etc. - is more precise and efficient.

16. An overall increase in moral: Optimum morale is attained when your people feel good about and believe in: themselves, their company, their product and their market place. One of the most important benefits of successful implementation an effective sale process is sustainable improvement in all of these areas.

The 10 Most Common Sales Force Hiring Mistakes

Hiring superstar sales talent is a lot easier than your managers will tell you. Their problem: they think hiring sales people is the same as hiring for other positions. Wrong. Sales selection requires a completely different process.

Here are the ten most common sales force-hiring mistakes and how to avoid them.

Mistake #1: Not making recruiting and retaining great sales talent your #1 business priority. Solution: Make this a significant goal for all your managers, and tie a good chunk of their performance bonus to the goal.

Mistake #2: Lacking a system for recruiting top talent from outside your industry. Solution: Create a hiring process for identifying top talent from industries with similar sales environments, and include an on-boarding program to cut ramp time. Example: Sellers who've sold conceptual financial services by calling on CEOs and presidents can ramp up to sell other conceptual services, like advertising or consulting.

Mistake #3: Hiring salespeople who can sell instead of those who *will* sell. The ONLY criterion for selecting superior sales talent is: Will they sell? Not "can they sell?" Sales teams are full of imposters who know how to sell, but won't.

Mistake #4.: Not knowing how to IDENTIFY superstar sales candidates. Solution: Pick the best sales people in your industry, or your company and perform a benchmark evaluation of the behaviors, attitudes, skills and environmental fit to make them champions.

Mistake #5: Hiring managers conduct traditional interviews, and fail to ask the right questions to unmask the "real" candidate. Solution: Conduct audition interviews, which simulate the tough environment to which a real prospect would subject them.

Mistake #6: Hiring to availability instead of to excellence. Solution: Hold your hiring managers accountable to hiring only "A" players.

Mistake #7: Hiring people based on "impressions" instead of hiring those they know will sell. Solution: Change your hiring criteria.

Mistake #8: Failing to learn the hidden weaknesses that neutralize selling skills. Solution: Learn how to spot them.

Mistake #9: Failing to measure and reward your employees for referring great candidate employees. Solution: Make it a priority. Set goals for candidate referrals. Pay handsomely, half on hire, half six months later.

Mistake #10: Advertising for positions, instead of for people. Solution: The magic is to write ads to describe your superstar. How? Write ads that cause superstars to remark upon reading: "That's me." Example:

Who Else Wants to Be a Millionaire?

Wish you could be a part of a team of professional people doing professional things in a professional way? Are you better than the average sales person, and are you tired of doing more and earning less? Can you cold call CEOs, Presidents and Owners of small to medium sized businesses selling conceptual services people need but do not want? Can you close orders in one to two calls for $50-$200k. Have you earned over $100k in straight commissions, and do you want a lifestyle that demands at least three times that? Do you want to retire a millionaire with the time to enjoy it? If this is you, you'd better call fast, because we're on a fast track and we're looking for runners. Call 800-250-3146.

....

You Can't Shrink Your Way To Excellence

So the economy has been in the tank and orders aren't coming in fast enough. Contracts are being cancelled, and salespeople are quickly learning that selling is more than showing up and taking orders. So what do most managers do? Take out the knife and cut back. When that doesn't work they cut back some more. While it may seem prudent and good business to cut costs where you can, this approach can have disastrous consequences when it is applied to the sales force. Why?

Consider this: If the average salesperson brings in 10 to 15 times their compensation in sales, why would we want FEWER of them? Other than marketing, sales is the only area that generates revenue for a company. Not accounting, administration, HR, not any other department. When a company cuts back on hiring, recruiting or training sales people they effectively limit their future.

Your financial people, who do not understand or appreciate the sales role, will argue that you should cut anywhere you can. Fine. If you must cut, cut everything else but not the sales force.

In this economy, you must put MORE salespeople to work, not less and you must provide MORE training, not less. Initiate MORE accountability, not less.

INCREASE recruiting efforts, not reduce them.

Companies must perform their way to excellence. It takes work to grow and take market share by out-hustling, out-strategizing and out-recruiting your competitors. Most managers resist this because the left side of their brain is addicted to quick fixes, while the right side of their brain is on a starvation diet.

If sales are flat, or worse, down from your goals and projections, INCREASE the sales effort and do not tighten the belt in the sales department. Have your sales organization evaluated, find out who has the ability to become more effective and give them the training they'll need to reach their fullest potential.

As a manager, give yourself a gut-check and decide if you want to follow the herd, or get up front and lead. Are you content to merrily co-exist in your market, or do you have the commitment to step up and dominate it with bold strategies and solid execution?

Not Everyone Is Trainable

Companies waste millions of dollars each year sending people to sales training. Many of these people don't want to be there, will not benefit from being there, and should really be doing something else with their time.

When salespeople under perform, training is not always the magic cure. So instead of hiring warm bodies and then trying to train them, companies would do well to concentrate their resources on developing better hiring and recruiting practices. This would result in hiring stronger salespeople who could benefit from training.

There is an old southern expression that says it best, "you can't make a silk purse out of a sow's ear." So true.

According to Dave Kurlan's blog post on hiring efficiency, only 15% of sales candidates that are tested by his company pass the pre-hire screening test, and are recommended for hire. These numbers are in line with Herb Greenberg's numbers that state that only of 20% of the people now selling has the emotional and psychological talents to be top performers. Both of these numbers are in line with the Pareto Principle.

In my study of sales, I have found that the normal bell shaped curve applies to sales organizations. This normal distribution can be understood by identifying the four kinds of performers within an organization. These four can be labeled A's, B's, C's and D's.

For training purposes these groups can be divided into two groups: The Trainables and The Non-Trainables.

The Trainables are: A's who are highly productive, motivated to grow and trainable and C's who are non-productive, but motivated and trainable.

The Non-Trainables are: B's who are highly productive, but are comfortable with their current level of income, have no motivation to grow, and are not receptive to training, and D's who are not productive, and have no potential for growth.

If we apply the normal bell shaped curve to a sales organization, we will find about 20% of the sales organization are A's, 60% are B's and C's and 20% are D's.

From a training standpoint, the only salepeople it makes sense to train are the A's and the C's who want to become A's – usually about half of this C group. The B's are not candidates for training unless and until they become uncomfortable with their current level of success. The D's are not trainable and should be replaced.

Using these numbers, on average, only about half of any sales organization, the A's and half of the C's will benefit from training.

When we work with companies to improve the sales process we usually find that improving the sales process involves a two pronged approach of identifying and training the trainables and implementing a more effective recruiting and hiring process to replace the non-productive, non-trainables.

....

What Kind of Sales People Do You Have Working for You and Do You Know How to Manage Each of Them

Like the optimistic goal of finding the perfect husband or wife, the hunt for the perfect Account Executive goes unfulfilled.

For as long as sales people have roamed the earth there have been "winners" and "losers." For just as long, sales managers have been searching for the elusive "perfect sales person."

Sales managers perspectives must change. Instead of looking for the perfect person, they must learn to identify and hire sales candidates that have the basic skills and talents to become successful, and then apply superior sales management practices to compensate for the short-comings new hires have. The ability to recognize, communicate, coach and motivate each of the four types of sales personalities will ultimately determine a manager's success.

Let's take a look at the four types of Account Executives and how to manage each:

Hunters

These types are resilient when it comes to rejection. They have a sense of urgency and close hard and fast. They push for the sale, collect the check and move on to the next kill. They're competitive, positive, high energy, dynamic, fast passed, results oriented and they have very high egos.

They are not good relationship builders, team players and are demanding.

They have a psychological need to convince others to their way of thinking and their greatest strength in selling is closing new business. They can be your biggest advocate or your worst nightmare.

Management Key: Have them stay out of the office and work on their own where they won't have to interact and upset the rest of the staff.

Farmers

Farmers have a retail sales mentality and would rather respond to customer requests than initiate contact. When they do respond it is in a low key-key friendly manner. They do not really consider themselves to be sales people. They take rejection very personally and spend a lot of their time trying to work through their feelings of rejection. Farmers will not cold call because they cannot psychologically tolerate rejection. They view cross selling or up selling as imposing on the customer. Their belief is that if someone wants to buy something they will initiate the contact. They value their customers and take wonderful care of existing clients. They are reliable order takers and make great customer service representatives.

Management Key: Give them accounts that require a lot of customer service and relationship building.

Account Penetrators

These sales people are superb long term relationship builders because they possess great patience. They are able to balance the sense of urgency to get new business with the patience to develop new relationships. Their emphasis is on creative problem solving and they excel in consultative selling environments.

They create customer loyalty because of their relationship skills. They are wonderful cross sellers and up sellers and will pursue those opportunities once they have penetrated an account.

Penetrators are political animals who can read who the players are and successfully navigate the political bureaucracy within organizations. They have boundless energy for socializing and networking and see themselves as consultants not sales people.

Their shortcomings are that they are not prospectors and will resist cold calling unless made to do so.

> **Management Key:** Give them prospects and accounts that typically have long sales cycles and multiple layers of decision making.

Charismatics

These folks seem to be living on the edge and almost out of control. They have limitless energy and are in a constant state of movement. They are great initiators of contact or action. They are excessive in every thing they do. They start lots of things but never seem to finish any of them. They are well liked, friendly, social, and outgoing. These folks are master prospectors and will burn up the phone lines and fill up the pipeline. They appear a lot like a Hunter except they are lacking in the ability to close.

They lack focus, are impulsive and overextend themselves to the point of exhaustion. They have a tendency to over promise what you can deliver because they think any thing is possible. They continually shoot themselves in the foot by being totally disorganized and are terrible time managers.

Their sales forecasts are often not worth the paper they are written on. They are the company leaders in pending files and deadwood and they are the mortal enemy of the accounting and traffic departments.

> **Management Key:** Provide strict accountability for their activity and provide plenty of structure and processes for them.

Each of these types of sales people need to be managed differently. A sales manager must not only be able to recognize who she has working for her but she must know how to manage each style and temperament for maximum performance. The management style that works well for one of these types will not work for the others. In order to become more effective, sales managers need to spend time upgrading their knowledge and skills of psychological typing, human relations, coaching and communication. Sadly, most of them are unwilling to do so.

Why Do So Many Small Businesses Eventually Fail

Each year there are over 1,000,000 small businesses started in North America. 800,000 of these fail in the first five years. Of those 200,000 that make it past five years 160,000 fail in the next five years says, Michael Gerber, the author of the E-Myth, one of the top 5 best selling business books of all time.

Recently, I participated in a conference call with Michael Gerber who said, "I know more about small business than any human on the planet". It would be hard to disagree with a man who has consulted with over 10,000 small businesses since 1977.

In this conference call, he said the biggest problem small business owners have is that they are too busy "doing it, doing it, doing it" to really develop the systems that are necessary to run their businesses without them. He went on to say that owners of businesses who don't have systems to run their businesses without them don't really own a business. They own a job. He further stated that in this scenario the owner is not really building an asset to sell because no investor wants to buy a job.

On this call, he mentioned that McDonald's is the classic and perhaps best example of a business that is run entirely on systems. These systems allow them to run a worldwide business that does hundreds of billions of dollars per year even though they have a 400% annual turnover rate and employee primarily teenage labor. Their secret? SYSTEMS RUN THE BUSINESS NOT PEOPLE. This reliance to systems is hugely successful and requires no day to day involvement from the franchise owner.

When questioned why small businesses fail he mentioned several reasons:

1. In most cases the owner got their start as a really good "doer of the thing" they are now in business to do.

He mentioned that most small business owners lack the full range of business skills necessary to effectively manage and run a high level organization. As owners they still think like technicians or sales people and as a result of this thinking they have not elevated their business management skills beyond that of a "doer".

2. Arrogance and Ignorance.

Because the owners are technically good at what they do they think they know how to run a business. However, most of them have had little if any formal business education other than running their own business, attending industry trade shows and modeling whatever is considered accepted "industry business practices". They suffer from the myopic "herd" mentality and lack innovation or imagination which is the currency of 21st century business leadership.

3. They don't realize that they are the primary obstacle to their business growth.

Instead of being open minded they think they have the answers. The reality is that they don't know what they don't know.

4. **They mistaken think that whatever business strategies and practices that worked in the past will work in the future.**

As a result, they make faulty business decisions about the future, fail to implement effective systems and their business falls further and further behind the change curve until lone day they wake up and realize that the world has changed and passed them by. By then it is usually too late.

Because of changing market conditions, increased competition and technology, the lack of systematic processes and methodologies that allowed a business to succeed previously will not be good enough to sustain it at its current level long term, much less take it to the next level.

As surely as the sun will rise tomorrow, change will happen in business. The only question is will a business owner proactively choose to embrace change or will they be forced to change by external circumstances?

To quote Jack Welch, the former CEO of General Electric, "when the change outside your business is greater than the change inside your business the end is in site

Why Is Change So Difficult

In my consulting practice the hardest thing to get clients to do is to change their behavior. While they logically agree —at the intellectual level—that they need to change things they seldom make the significant changes that would propel their business forward.

Before you start thinking you are different you must realize that they are you and you are they.

A Universal Truth

The human organism is resistant to change.

The body tries to maintain what physiologists call homeostasis. This is the physical state of equilibrium or status quo. The body is designed to operate in a very narrow range of physiological processes. The brain is no different.

We all refuse to change our ways for reasons that are often hard to articulate.

Until, that is, you begin looking at it from a scientific perspective. In the past few years, improvements in have allowed researchers to track the energy of a thought coursing through the brain in much the same way that they can track blood flowing through the circulatory system. Watching different areas of the brain light up in response to specific thoughts has brought a new understanding to our response to change.

The major neuroimaging techniques used research are positron emission tomography (PET), single photon emission computed tomography (SPECT), and magnetic resonance imaging (MRI), along with electro-encephalography (EEG), an earlier technique for monitoring brain activity. Advances in all these techniques are enabling scientists to produce remarkably detailed computer-screen images of brain structures and to observe neurochemical changes that occur in the brain as it processes information or responds to various stimuli.

These brain analysis technologies show that our responses to change are predictable and universal. From a neurological perspective, we all respond to change in the same way: We try to avoid it.

Why Change Is Painful

Change creates psychological stress.

Change engages the prefrontal cortex, the conscious part of the brain that is responsible for judgment, planning and decision making. The prefrontal cortex is like RAM memory in a PC. It is fast and agile, able to hold multiple threads of logic at once to enable quick calculations. But like RAM, the prefrontal cortex's capacity is finite—it can deal comfortably with only a handful of concepts before becoming overloaded. When it becomes overloaded it generates a palpable sense of discomfort, anxiety, fatigue, and frustration.

Like a computer the brain prefers to run off its hard drive or basal ganglia, which has a much larger storage capacity. This is the part of the brain that stores the hardwired memories and habits that dominate our daily lives.

"Most of the time the basal ganglia are more or less running the show," says Jeffrey M. Schwartz, research psychiatrist at the School of Medicine at the University of California at Los Angeles. "It controls habit-based behavior that we don't have to think about doing."

In a sense, it is the basal ganglia that keeps us in that very narrow range called our comfort zone. If you want to make changes in your life you must realize that every change comes with a certain amount of psychological stress. The bigger the change the bigger the stress. Now you know why so few people are willing to consciously embrace change.

Six Human Motivators

What's Inside Top Performing Sales People?

What is it that motivates humans to take action? What is the source of their desire to become involved in or to avoid certain activities? What motivates humans to do what they do?

The answer to being effective, satisfied and personally fulfilled lies deep within a unique set of personal interests, attitudes and values.

Defining Attitudes

In 1928, Eduard Spranger wrote "Types of Men." In it he identified six major attitudes or worldviews. These attitudes are windows through which we view the world and seek fulfillment in our lives. If we are participating in a discussion, activity or career that is in alignment with our attitudes, we will value the experience and excel. Conversely, if we are in a conversation, activity or career that is in conflict with our dominant attitudes, we will be indifferent or even negative toward the experience, possibly causing stress.

The Six Attitudes

Theoretical: The primary drive with this value is the discovery of TRUTH. In pursuit of this value, an individual takes a cognitive or intellectual attitude. Since the interests of the theoretical person are empirical, critical and rational, the person appears to be an intellectual. The chief aim of this attitude in life is to order and systematize knowledge for the sake of knowledge.

Utilitarian: The Utilitarian attitude is a characteristic interest in money and what is useful. An individual with a high Utilitarian attitude wants to have the security that money brings not only for themselves, but for their present and future family. This value includes the practical affairs of the business world - the production, marketing and consumption of goods, the use of credit, and the accumulation of tangible wealth. This type of individual is thoroughly practical and conforms well to the stereotype of the average American business person. A person with a high Utilitarian score is likely to have a high need to surpass others in wealth.

Aesthetic: A higher Aesthetic score indicates a relative interest in "form and harmony." Each experience is judged from the standpoint of grace, symmetry or fitness. Life may be regarded as a procession of events, and each is enjoyed for its own sake. A high score here does not necessarily mean that the individual has talents in creative artistry. It indicates a primary interest in the artistic episodes of life.

Social: Those who score very high in this value have an inherent love of people. The social person prizes other people and is, therefore, kind, sympathetic and unselfish. They are likely to find the Theoretical, Utilitarian and Aesthetic attitudes cold and inhuman. Compared to the Individualistic value, the Social person regards helping others as the only suitable form for human relationships. Research into this value indicates that in its purest form, the Social interest is selfless.

Individualistic: The primary interest for this value is POWER, not necessarily politics. Research studies indicate that leaders in most fields have a high power value. Since competition and struggle play a large part in all areas of life, many philosophers have seen power as the most universal and most fundamental of motives. There are, however, certain personalities in whom the desire for direct expression of this motive is uppermost; who wish, above all, for personal power, influence and renown.

Traditional: The highest interest for this value may be called "unity," "order," or "tradition." Individuals with high scores in this value seek a system for living. This system can be found in such things as religion, conservatism or any authority that has defined rules, regulations and principles for living.

In a ground breaking study Bill Bonnstetter, President of Target Training International, Ltd. in Scottsdale, Arizona and Frank Scheelen of the The Scheelen Institute, Waldshut-Tiengen, Germany confirmed that (1) top performing sales people around the world are similar and (2) that attitudes or motivations are more important than behavioral style or personality.

In this study participants were given two validated psychometric assessments: (1) the DISC - a behavioral style analysis or personality assessment and (2) the PIAV - a Personal Interest, Values and Attitude assessment.

In this study they concluded that most if not all personality types can sell. However, the most remarkable aspect of their study was the fact that seventy-one (71) percent of the top performing salespeople in 492 companies in Germany and 178 companies in the United States had Ultilitarian motivation as their top motivator. The conclusion from this study is that when it comes to top performing sales people motivation is more important than personality hands down.

....

Where Are All of the Job Applicants

The nation's first baby boomer, Kathleen Casey-Kirschling, a former teacher from New Jersey applied for Social Security Monday, the start of an avalanche of applications from the post-World War II generation.

Casey-Kirschling was born one second after midnight on Jan. 1, 1946, making her the first baby boomer -- a generation of nearly 80 million born from 1946 to 1964.

In 2007 Baby Boomers represent nearly one- half of the U.S. work force. The number of workers 55 and older is growing four times faster that the work force as a whole. As the baby-boomer generation retires from the U.S. work force, companies will have to cope with the fact that Generation X's, who were born between 1964 and 1982 and number only 44 million, will not be able to fill the talent gap.

What does all of this mean for you or the company you own or work for?

If you are an employee it means that there will be an increasing demand and opportunity for your skills. If you are a hiring manager or business owner it means you are going to find it more and more difficult to find and retain good employees.

What can you do to maximize the talent acquisition and minimize the talent drain:

- Implement extensive communication and relationship building skills training for the management team

- Institute a training program that helps employees further their technical, personal and communication skills

- Improve personal and communication skills among all employees

- Provide coaching and career path development opportunities for key employees

- Make work fun

- Provide a flexible work schedule

- Allow employees to work remotely or from home

- Learn what motivates each individual employee and provide proper motivation and management

The astute manager realizes that their best customers are in fact their employees...

...and how they treat these "internal customers" is how these internal customers will treat the external customers / buyers.

CHAPTER 7: GOALS

....

If You Don't Know Where You Are Going.....

Imagine going up to the airline ticket counter and telling the ticket agent you would like to purchase a ticket to go on a wonderful vacation, but you aren't sure where you want to go or when you want to go. What do you think their response would be? Maybe something like *"well when you figure out where you want to go and when you want to go come back and I'll help you. Now please step aside so I can help the next person in line."*

In Lewis Carol's *Alice in Wonderland* there is a wonderful passage where the Cheshire cat addresses this same issue by saying to Alice, *"if you don't know where you are going any road will take you there."*

In my coaching practice the single biggest issue I am presented with is that business owners and salespeople don't know the answer to the questions...

"...where do you want your business to be and when do you want it to be there?"

When I ask these questions the answers I hear are things like: "*I want to make more sales/money, or I want my business to do better or we want to grow our sales and profits.*"

Those answers are not good enough because they are vague, hazy, non specific or measurable. Consequently, they are not realistic or attainable. Before you start trying to figure out how you must first answer the question where and why. Failing to do this, your efforts and activity will produce the same results as a dog chasing his tail.

How do you begin this process? You begin by spending some quality time developing a blueprint for your future.

Start by thinking of how you would like to be spending your time. Of all the kinds of work you could be doing, what do you want to do the most? How many hours do you want to work each week, and how would you like to divide up your working time? Then think about what kind of people you would like to interact with. Who are your ideal clients, customers, colleagues and employees? Next imagine the physical environment in which you would like your business to operate. What would it look like? How large a space would you want? What would it look and feel like? What level of business would you have? How much revenue and profits? How many clients, billable hours etc.

would you have? What would be the mix of clients or services that you would provide?

Write your answers in present tense. Don't worry if your picture is a little fuzzy or you can't answer all of the questions. You are striving for process not perfection. This process will help you develop the focus necessary to achieve your hearts desire. It takes a lot of time and effort, and some deep soul searching. It is not easy. That is why only 3% percent of people will do it.

You have a choice. You can consciously choose to be one of the 3% that pursues personal excellence or by default you will become part of the 97% mass of humanity that spends their life in mediocrity. I hope you choose to become one of the 3%.

Are You Living an Intentional Life

Are you living intentionally or by accident? Are you proactive or reactive? Do you find yourself out of control and feel that you are being sweep up in a vortex that is beyond your control?

Most people are living their life by accident. They are stumbling through life as if they are a pebble being swept downstream by a current they cannot control. They feel powerless and out of control. They feel helpless and victimized by circumstances.

This sense of helplessness has horrendous consequences. Today there are more personal bankruptcies that at any point in history. The use of antidepressants is epidemic. Libido enhancing commercials dominate the Super Bowl ads. People are whacked out.

Why?

One of the reasons is that individuals have given up the idea of personal responsibility. They have abandoned the idea that "happiness is an inside job" Instead of looking inwardly for direction and meaning in life they have given up and now look outwardly to the government, the company, their parents or employers for their direction. This is easier than looking in the mirror and asking hard questions such as "Why am I here? What do I really want? Or what do I need to change about myself?

Why don 't we talk about these things openly like we talk about sports or politics? Perhaps it is because we don't want to accept the ultimate truth that we are who we are and where we are because of what we have either done or not done in our life. It's tough to admit that we not someone else or something else is responsible for our circumstances in life.

People who live intentionally take ultimate responsibility for everything in their life. They refuse to make excuses or rationalize their situation. They accept that the problems in their life are of their own doing. Once they accept this they get on with fixing what needs to be fixed in their life. It takes a lot of courage to do this. Unfortunately, most people don't have it.

You can either be part of your plan or you WILL become part of someone else's plan.

The choice is yours.

....

How To Get What You Really, Really, Really Want

It doesn't really matter what the economy is going to do. It doesn't matter if it is up or down. The key is what do you EXPECT. Salespeople don't get what they want but they do get what they expect. Sales, like life, is a self-fulfilling prophecy. Don't let others such as co-workers; the media, friends, family or anyone else set your expectations for you.

Here is a step-by-step plan to help you:

1. Determine what you want clearly and specifically

2. Determine the amount of prospecting activity that it will take to achieve this goal

3. Create a detailed, weekly plan to accomplish the activity

4. Commit to do "whatever it takes"

5. Track your activity and results

6. Analyze your results and make corrections to your plan

7. Start over at number 1

This is not hard to do but it does take commitment. It is also what separates the mediocre from the great. Choose to be great.

Begin With The End In Mind

Stephen Covey, author of *The Seven Habits of Highly Effective People* coined the phrase "Begin with the end in mind", What that means is you should have a blueprint for what you want your business to look like before you go out and start running helter skelter. Most salespeople have no long-term written business plan. They are too busy working on the urgency of making calls to spend time on the important things like designing their future.

If you go out and do tons and tons of cold calling prospecting behavior daily you have a job not a business. Most of the salespeople who are in the upper 5% in their industry have learned how to transition from cold calling to building a referral based business. There are very few of these top performers who do 100 plus cold calls daily.

I hear a lot of sales people and sales managers talk about "hitting the street or hitting the phones". That behavior may be acceptable for someone who is new and full of enthusiasm for selling. However, at some point banging on doors and dialing for dollars gets old. That's when people begin to question their commitment to selling. Why do you think so many people get out of selling? Even with a good approach people get tired hearing NO 50 to 100 times a day.

The object of this business of selling is not to see how many calls you can make and how many hours you can work but to see how much money you can put in the bank.

Without a doubt proper referral prospecting is the highest ROI of time and money. I urge you to cold call if you must but while you are doing it begin to learn how to gradually transition to more and more referrals. You will make more money, you will be less stressed and you will work fewer hours.

As You Begin The End Of The Quarter Here Are A Few Things To Think About!

What are you going to do between now and the end of the quarter? Here are some questions for you to ponder, reflect and hopefully act on.

1. How many prospects do you want to contact between now and quarter?

2. Based on your closing percentages, how many first time conversations will you need to have to hit your production goals? How many do you need per week?

3. How many names do you have on your written prospect list TODAY? (Hint – you need to have more than the answer to question number 2)

4. If you do not have enough names on your prospect list when will you sit down and complete this job?

5. What is your prospecting plan? You do have a written prospecting plan for the quarter don't you? Is it broken down into measurable, weekly activity?

6. How will you track and keep score of your activity?

7. Have you made daily appointments with yourself to prospect? Are they written in your calendar?

I urge you to sit down and devote some quality time to answer these questions and make a plan. After all, "In the absence of clearly defined goals and objective anything becomes acceptable".

You are better than that.

CHAPTER 8: STRATEGIES AND TECHNIQUES

Are Buyers Really Liars

Not long ago, I overheard a salesperson make a comment which – taken out of context – sounds appalling. He said, "buyers are liars." Whenever I hear something brief and incisive, I stop for a moment and think, "Truth? Or just a catchy rhyme?" This time, however, I had to admit: There is a bit of truth in what that salesperson said.

Don't misunderstand – buyers aren't bad people. But sometimes buyers and prospects mislead salespeople by not giving exact or complete information; they tell "little white lies".

There are many reasons why buyers mislead:

- Buyers don't want to give up control of the negotiations to the salesperson.

- They don't trust the salesperson.

- They don't feel comfortable with the salesperson.

- They don't want to feel like they're being bamboozled into buying something they really don't need or want.

- They don't want to be pressured.

- They don't want to give any information to a salesperson that could be used against them.

- They are skeptical and feel they always have to have their guard up.

Whatever the reasons, salespeople have trained buyers to feel this way.

Certainly the majority of salespeople want to solve they buyer's problems; however, most salespeople are cursed with the stereotypical image of the high pressure, fast talking, conniving salesperson who taints the credibility of all other salespeople.

Even though such salespeople represent only a small percentage, every one of us has been exposed to the kinds of sales tactics that ultimately create barriers between the buyer and the seller. Such slick sales gimmicks are not the answer.

The truly professional salesperson uses non-pressure techniques to help buyers discover their reasons for buying.

There are three reasons why people buy. First, **"People like to buy... but they don't like to be sold."** Most sales training teaches the theory of educating the buyer on product knowledge. But when a salesperson tries to sell features and benefits without understanding the true reasons why a customer buys, the barriers go up and the customer resists. Traditional sales training also encourages people to "ask for the order". But there is only one person who can ask for the order: the customer. That's why *human behavior-based sales training* teaches a discovery system that shows you how to use your questioning skills to encourage customers to determine their buying motive for themselves – which then leads customers to ask for the order.

The second reason why people buy is, **"People like to buy from people they are comfortable with and who are like them."**

Have you ever been on that sales call when the customer felt comfortable with you, the chemistry between you was the same, and there was an emotional bond between you? Wouldn't it be great to reproduce that same feeling on *every* sales call? Why can't we do that? Salespeople have to deal with so many different personalities that it's impossible to bond with everyone they meet. You only have so many hours in the day to get in front of potential buyers, and getting there is the hardest part of the sale. If you are depending on finding a buyer more like yourself, you won't close many sales.

Learning behavior skills that make us appear to be more like the buyer is rarely taught in any sales training course. Yet these skills are easy to learn, and if they become part of your selling process people will feel more comfortable with you because they believe you are more like them.

The third and final reason why people buy is, **"People buy *emotionally*; they make decisions *intellectually*."**

Most of the time, salespeople spend their energy selling features and benefits. They rarely understand the buyer's emotional needs, which are rooted in three basic emotions: pleasure, fear, and pain avoidance. Because the salesperson spends so much time on the intellectual side of the sale, the buyer responds with intellectual smoke screens such as, "I'll think it over," "We will get back to you," or "Call me next week." If you can get the buyer emotionally involved in the selling process, you will soon learn the truth: Either "Yes, we will do business with you," or "No, we won't do business with you." Anything in between is purely a smoke screen and proves that even though the salesperson is talking, the buyer isn't listening.

Knowing the features and benefits of your products and services is important; but salespeople have to develop the questioning skills to get the buyer to discover the emotional reasons why they should buy the solution that is being presented to them. When the buyer discovers – really *feels* – how your products and services can help him, the sale is complete.

If your present selling system doesn't address the three reasons why prospects buy, find a selling system that will help the customer discover that you have the answers to their problems, issues and concerns. Buyers are liars? In a way, yes…but they have their reasons!

Transactional Buyers vs. Relationship Buyers

There are two types of buyers: transactional and relational. Transactional buyers are concerned about today's purchase. They do a lot of research investigating the product they are considering buying and consider himself or herself a product expert. They are not as concerned about service, trust or relationship. They are concerned primarily about price and terms. They enjoy negotiating and trying to extract as many concessions out of the salesperson as possible. They see what they are doing as a game. A game where they win and the salesperson loses. They will "milk" the salesperson for free information, technical data, etc. Because of their "I win you lose" approach they have no loyalty. They are a salesperson's worst nightmare.

Relationship Buyers consider today's transaction as one in a series of many. They do not enjoy playing the "shopping game." They don't enjoy comparison shopping or negotiating. They are looking for a Business Partner or Trusted Advisor who is an expert that they can trust. Once they find someone they trust they are loyal and tend to be the best repeat customers. While relational buyers consider the money they also realize that their time is better spent doing something other than shopping around. Because of their "I win and you win" orientation they are honest, open and pleasant to deal with.

Intentionally or unwittingly, companies will target either the transactional or relationship buyer. Who is your company targeting? What kind of business are you building?

....

Understanding The Cast of Characters

In a complex sale, one in which there is more than one decision maker, you have four types of buyers: the Economic Buyer, the Technical Buyer, the End User and the Coach. Each of them has their role to play. The EB is concerned with the bottom line. The TB is concerned with product performance. The EU is concerned with how will this make my job easier or better. The Coach is concerned with helping you get the business. (They are your inside salesperson.)

All four of these have the capacity of "killing " the deal. All four roles can consist of individuals or groups. Some of the players may serve in more than one role and each of them have to be sold individually. Each of them has different "pains" or concerns. In order to make the sale the sales person has to: identify whom the players are, develop relationships with each of them, approach and sell to each one individually and collectively.

Failing to do this is dangerous and costly. The fallacy sales people make in situations like this is to focus on product and price. In complex selling it is NEVER about product or price. It is about process and relationship. This is the art of Strategic Selling. It is what separates the great producers from the good producers.

....

Crises or Opportunity

Crisis and opportunity are two sides of the same coin that exist simultaneously. When one exists so does the other. They are inseparable.

We hear a lot about cutbacks, layoffs, slowdowns and recession. The popular press loves bad news. Why? Because bad news always sells better than good news. Those who get a steady diet of electronic or print news are bound to feel depressed. It is impossible to be fed this stuff without it influencing one's attitude.

During the economic boom of the nineties, business was easy and few salespeople were really "put to the test." Because the nineties were one of the most prosperous decades in our history most salespeople that have less than ten years experience have never experienced selling in a recession.

THE RULES HAVE CHANGED.

As things tighten up, those companies with stagnate and ineffective sales forces will quickly become frustrated with their inability to sell and compete effectively. And the salespeople, many of whom have never seen a tough market, will get more frustrated and less productive. A great many of them will leave the profession.

What's the answer? Quit listening to the nay Sayers of this world. Turn off the TV. Quit reading garbage that affects your attitude. Go to work on developing an abundant mentality. Give thanks for what you do have. Redouble your efforts to improve your selling skills.

There are two ways to look at it. Is the glass half full or half empty? Those who see it as half full, see a great opportunity to take market share from the lazy and unskilled sales people they compete against. These current conditions will really separate the true sales professionals from the pitchmen and product peddlers who are always abundant during the easy times. I for one will be glad to see it happen.

....

What Happens Next?

Several times recently I have had conversations with clients who were unclear about what the next step in the sales process was. They find themselves leaving sales calls with unclear expectations as to what happens next and when it is to happen. This happens in part because they make assumptions and allow prospects to be vague about their intentions and decisions.

To prevent this from happening, you must be able to clearly answer the question "What happens next and when"? If you are not sure then

ASK! Before you leave a call learn the specifics of the next step in the process, gain mutual agreement from your prospect about the next step, and then schedule a specific time to follow up on what has been agreed to. This one technique will eliminate wasted time by at least 25%.

....

Ten Sales Basics

Even if you think you're well versed in the selling basics, it's important to keep your skills razor sharp. Sales fundamentals like listening and needs analysis may make the difference between closing and losing, so don't assume that a refresher course in the basis is beneath your level of expertise. These 10 reminders will keep your skills polished and form a strong selling foundation for career-long success.

1. Listen intently. The 80/20 rule bears repeating: Spend 80 percent of your time listening, and only 20 percent talking. You're there to serve your customer's needs, but you won't be able to if you don't stop talking long enough to uncover them. Ask a lot of questions, and take notes on the answers to force you to listen carefully and help ensure that you remember important points of the conversation. Sit on the edge of your seat, and be fascinated by what your prospects have to say – a big sale may be riding on every word.

2. Ask questions first, present later. If your presentation doesn't highlight the features or benefits your prospects are interested

in, it probably won't convince them to buy. Make sure you understand their needs, wants, expectations and feelings 100 percent so that your presentation hits all of their hot buttons. Ask questions first to ensure that you don't share all your good news on page one – it may help build your prospect's trust by showing them that their needs come before your desire to sell to them.

3. Uncover needs – don't presume them. Just as no competent doctor prescribes treatment before thoroughly examining a patient, you should let your prospects tell you what they need instead of assuming that you already know. Should you make product or service recommendations without consulting them, they may question your competence and intentions. Remember – your prospects know themselves and their businesses best. Give them a chance to share that knowledge with you to benefit you both.

4. Ask for a budget range. Once you and your prospects know how much they can spend, both of you can consider a buying decision more seriously. Assure prospects that you'll do your best for them regardless of the size of their budget. When you've proven your honesty and reliability with a small order, your customers may reward you with more and bigger ones. If your prospect seems uncomfortable discussing money, ask for a ballpark figure off the record, and work from there.

5. Talk to the decision maker. Who wants to make a convincing presentation to an enthusiastic prospect who has no purchasing power? Presentations demand a lot of work and time, so make sure you present only to those who can reward

your effort with a sale. It may take longer to reach upper management, but trying to sell to anyone else simply wastes time – yours and theirs. Instead of presenting to the wrong people, spend your time building rapport with gatekeepers who hold the key to the decision maker's office and your next sale.

6. Build rapport without going overboard. Salespeople who try too hard to make friends of their prospects may be doing more harm than good. Most prospects want a salesperson who will be an informative industry resource, problem solver and reliable business partner – not a golfing buddy. Stick to impressing prospects with your honesty and expertise instead of your winning personality. If you notice a golf trophy or college pennant you can relate to, talk about it for two minutes, then move on to the real purpose of your call.

7. Answer all unspoken objections and questions. When customers voice concerns be brutally honest with them about the pros and cons of your product or service. Every product or service has limitations. Being brutally honest with your buyer will build great trust and credibility and reduce their fear and anxiety about.

8. Customize the sale. We all like to be treated like the special, unique individuals that we are, so tailor your selling style to suit each of your prospects. To keep them happy and comfortable, observe their personality and character closely, and then conduct yourself accordingly. Use such rapport-building phrases as "That's interesting," "Tell me more" and "You're right." The more your customers feel like the center

of your attention, the more likely they are to return for more of the VIP treatment.

9. Go with the flow. Few people really like to be sold, and fewer still enjoy being manipulated. Your desire to close a sale is secondary to your customers' needs – make sure you can really help the prospects you target. When your product or service truly solves a problem, you shouldn't have to manipulate the buyer into a purchase. The hard sell usually only raises the prospect's defenses. Instead, take greater control of the sale by turning some of it over to the customer.

10. Have a selling system. Make sure you have a proven system that helps you generate prospects, set appointments, close sales and provide quality, consistent follow-up service. When problems arise, your system will simplify diagnosing and treating them.

....

Are You Asking The Right Questions?

Prospects and customers have two frequent complaints about salespeople. The first, they talk too much. The second, they don't listen very well. Many salespeople agree they need to be better listeners. Some, in fact, are learning to become *active* listeners.

Becoming an active listener, however, doesn't ensure that you will improve the results of your selling efforts. The information you are now *actively* gathering must be sufficient and appropriate for you to qualify or disqualify your prospect and, if necessary, put together the correct presentation.

In order to hear the right information, you must stop prematurely giving out information and instead, ask questions. And, you must ask the right questions – ones that allow you to get an accurate picture of your prospect's needs, wants and situation.

You must be able to determine exactly what your prospect is trying to achieve. You must also determine why they are trying to achieve it. *Specifically,* why? What has kept them from that achievement so far? What potential roadblocks lie ahead? What are the benefits of succeeding in their goal? What are the consequences of failing? How would success or failure affect them?

Asking questions to uncover this information accomplishes two things; it allows you to better assess the situation and determine if there is a real opportunity for you, and perhaps more importantly, it gives the prospect an opportunity to crystallize and clarify his or her thinking.

Prospects often think they have a clear picture of a solution until they are asked to pick the problem apart and examine it in greater depth. Your questions must facilitate that process.

You must keep "picking away" at the problem with your questions until the real source of the problem is revealed. Questions and responses such as: "Why is that?" " How so? " "And...?" " Like...?" "What else?" "Another view might be...?" should be part of your questioning

191

arsenal. Remember, your objective is to keep the prospect talking. If they are talking, you won't be.

Using the *newspaper story* approach – who, what, where, why, when and how – to pick apart the problem may be helpful:

- Who is experiencing the problem? Who else? Who is affected by it?

- What specifically is the problem? What are the underlying causes? What did you do? What else do you want to add? What happens if you don't solve the problem?

- Where in the organization does the problem exist?

- Why specifically does the problem exist?

- When did the problem first become evident?

- When did they first decide to do something about it?

- How will they deal with the problem now?

- How long before they will give up?

....

Are You Really Listening?

Asking your prospect all the correct questions is wasted if you don't really hear what they are saying, whether expressed directly in words or more subtly in tones or partial hints. Do you hear everything that is being said? Do you understand it completely?

Being a good listener requires more than just keeping quiet while the other person is talking. Listening well is a difficult skill, but it can be mastered. Here are some tips on how to become a more effective listener.

- **Listen proactively.** There is more to listening than just passively hearing the words someone is speaking. One way to make sure you focus on what the person is saying is to "jump ahead", i.e., anticipate what the person is going to say next or the conclusion he or she is about to make. This keeps you mentally involved and thinking. (Your prospect has told you that his company has lost several salespeople over the year. He has talked about the cost of recruiting new people and the time it takes to get them up to speed and producing. How might you anticipate the following sentence will end? "I guess the greatest negative impact on the bottom line has been ____.")

- **Become personally absorbed in what is being said.** You can't listen effectively if you are only "going through the motions." Even less than absorbing information can be interesting. Every subject has <u>some</u> interesting angle, some impact on you or something you can learn. In order to uncover these elements, you must first abandon your prejudiced or preconceived ideas. If you enter into a conversation with the notion that the other person has nothing of interest or importance to say, you will miss what is important. Try to relate to the unrelated. Ask yourself how what the person is saying relates to other situations or experiences.

- **Make a concerted effort to listen.** Don't get distracted. Don't let trivial things like the speaker's appearance or random noises divert your attention from what they are saying. Listen to the speaker's whole sentence. Listen not only for content, but context. Anytime you catch yourself being distracted by something that draws your attention away from the speaker's words, make a conscious effort to focus back on the words.

- **Focus on what the speaker is trying to say.** Only 10% of what most speakers say is crucial. The rest is for illustration, explanation or transition. Focus in on the basic message. Try to pinpoint the main ideas the person is expressing. Ask yourself what the speaker is trying to say. If you're not sure, ask, "Bill, I believe what I heard is … Am I on track?"

- **Listen with your "gut".** The speaker's tone and body language will impart meaning. These subtle clues are more quickly picked up by the unconscious mind and leave us with a particular feeling about the speaker. The next time you are left with a feeling about someone after a conversation

– they are sincere, they are hiding something, they can't be trusted, etc. – it is just a sign that your unconscious mind has put two and two together and come up with an evaluation.

- **Understand what is being said.** Keep asking yourself if you understand what is being said. If you don't, ask for clarification – and keep asking until you are sure you fully understand. "Bill, I'm not sure I understand how…relates to… can you help me out?" What you don't understand, you can't recall. Additionally, if you don't understand what is being said, your mind is more likely to wander and your listening effectiveness diminishes.

- **Offer an intelligent comment.** To keep your active attention on what is being said, get involved. If the situation permits, offer your own perspective on what is being said. Ask a question or relate a relevant story that reinforces what the person is saying, or perhaps, represents a different point of view.

Been There Done That

You know the drill. You meet with a prospect and immediately they want you to spill your guts about what you do, how you do it, who you do it with and how much you do it for. They want you to do this and yet they are unwilling to share with you what their problems are, how much money they have budgeted and how they go about making decisions.

Why does this happen and more importantly, how do you prevent it from happening to begin with? The why part is easy to explain. Ignorant managers have taught salespeople that "sales is a numbers game" and that the more proposals they give the more sales they make. Consequently, they run all over the planet puking, vomiting and pitching product information to anyone who will fog a mirror. The result of this is that prospects have been conditioned that they should receive and are entitled to a "free education" from salespeople. So when you show up they expect you to jump through hoops and spill your guts like the last incompetent peddler.

How do you stop this? First you make a decision to stop doing it. Secondly, when you meet with a prospect establish some Rules of Engagement. This amounts to setting an agenda as to what will be discussed and in what order it will be discussed. As part of this process you must tell your prospect that you are not there to pitch product, give a quote or give a demo or presentation. You tell them that you are there to conduct an evaluation or their situation much like what a physician would do and that like a physician, you don't make diagnosis or write prescriptions until you have done a thorough examination. If your prospect resists letting you conduct an evaluation and insists that you give them a "quote or proposal" you politely get up and leave. That way you avoid wasting your time and theirs. It takes guts to do this but in the long run you will be better off.

....

Gaining Trust By Reading The Prospects Mind

According to Joseph E. LeDoux, Ph.D., a world-renowned neuroscientist at New York University, trust is a social emotion. It is the ability to put yourself in the mind of another and predict what they are thinking or what they will do. Psychologists call this the "theory of mind". To provoke trust, a sales person has to be able to put himself in the mind of the prospect and then perform to the expectation of the prospect. The more "predictable" a salesperson performs to the prospect's expectation the better the prospect feels. Therefore, a sales person who doesn't startle prospects with unexpected behaviors will do better and sell more.

How good are you at reading prospects and responding to what they need and expect?

....

How Do You Develop Loyal Clients

While the use of negative emotions is a desirable tactic to close a sale, it is not a desirable tactic to develop client loyalty.

> If you want to develop loyal clients you must learn to develop a positive emotional relationship with them.

This is more than being friendly or nice. It involves connecting with them on a deep positive emotional level.

According to Barbara Fredrickson, Ph.D., a research psychologist at the University of Michigan, and a vanguard in the field of Positive Psychology, "when people feel like they're being recognized as a human being on the other side of a transaction, as opposed to *being* the transaction, then they have a more positive response." Once someone experiences that feeling or emotion they tend to seek reinforcement from the person they associate with that emotion. This in turns builds loyalty to that person.

So how do you do this in a business environment? "Go out of your way to connect with people on a human level. Provide a service that's valuable, one that makes people think that the fit is so right that it's almost a gift …… make it your duty to go above and beyond the call of duty. And when people sense that one organization is doing that more often than others, that's what will create loyalty and engagement", says Fredrickson.

If you connect with your clients not only will they be more loyal they will go out of their way to do business with you even if they have to pay more for your service.

....

Quit Vomiting On Your Prospects

William James, the father of modern psychology, taught us that the number one need of human beings is not to understand but to be understood. You will be enormously successful if this is also the number one need that you fill in your selling process.

Your prospects will not be inclined to listen or care what you have to say until they have unloaded what's on their mind. Once they have the chance to "get it all out", they will then be ready to listen - and more importantly - ready to be sold.

Two Ears One Mouth

As salespeople, we have stores of helpful information to share. Often times, we can't wait to jump in and blurt out our wisdom and knowledge. The fact is that just has to wait. Instead of talking endlessly about what we do, how we do it and with whom we do it, we would be wise to learn how to ask questions that draw out the issues or concerns that our prospect has. Only when we fully understand what they are experiencing can we offer an intelligent solution.

Take stock of your process. Are you asking questions and gaining insight to prospects problems and concerns or are you "showing up and throwing up"?

What Motivates Prospects
To Make A Decision

Perhaps the answer to this question can be found from Barbara Fredrickson, Ph.D., a research psychologist at the University of Michigan, and a vanguard in the field of Positive Psychology.

According to Fredrickson negative emotions get people to act in particular ways or what she calls "specific action tendencies". Most of us know this as fight or flight. In essence, we have been biologically programmed by evolution to take action when we perceive danger or feel threatened. "Positive emotions don't necessarily narrow people toward a specific action like negative emotions do", says Fredrickson.

What does this have to do with selling? If you want to get a prospect to take action and buy your product or service you are more likely to succeed if you find a prospect that is experiencing a negative emotion. Negative emotions include things like losing money or time, loss of productivity, high employee turnover, etc. The one thing that all of these have in common is that they all relate to loss of something. Fear of loss (negative emotion) is a more powerful short-term motivator of human behavior than is the desire (positive emotion) for gain.

Think about it. When do people go to a physician? When they feel great and want to learn how to enhance (positive) their health or when they are in "pain" (negative) and want to get rid of their "pain"? Same thing when it comes to filing income tax returns. Over one million taxpayers wait until April 14th to file their taxes. Why? Fear of having to pay a penalty if they don't?

Become obsessed with finding "pain". If you do you will increase your income, shorten your sales cycle and have more fun selling.

....

Repositioning Your Competitor's Strength

Stop attacking your competition's weaknesses. Their clients did not buy from the because of these weaknesses. They bought from them because of their strengths. If you are going to take market share from your competition you need a new Direct Strategy. This strategy comes from a marketing book entitled *Positioning* by Jack Trout and Al Reiss:

Here is how it works:

    Step 1:   *Determine the strength of your competitor's position.*

    Step 2:   *Find a weakness in the leader's strength.*

    Step 3:   *Reposition their strength into a weakness.*

    Step 4:   *Launch your attack there, on as narrow a front as possible.*

    Step 5:   *Attack major weaknesses.*

Step 6:   *Make major weaknesses your strength.*

The strategy to attack the competitor's strength may seem to fly in the face of business logic. First, keep in mind that you won't take a significant number of clients away from your competitors by always attacking their weaknesses. Why? Because clients didn't buy from your competitor because of their weaknesses, they bought based on their strengths. Finding the weakness in their strength will provide you with your advantage over your competition, but it will also make you very attractive to the client. Here are a couple of examples of how this has worked:

Example #1

A real easy way to explain this is to see how Scope used this to take market share away from Listerine. For years Listerine dominated the mouthwash market. Their strength: Listerine mouthwash kills germs (Step 1). Scope found the weakness in the strength (Step 2), and repositioned that strength into a weakness (Step 3). Then they attacked on the narrowest front possible (Step 4). Scope attacked Listerine with an advertising campaign: "If you are tired of medicine breath, try Scope." They repositioned Listerine's strength into a weakness. It was a tremendous marketing success. For years competitors tried to take market share from Listerine and failed. Only when Listerine's strength became a weakness did they lose market share.

Example #2

When F.W. Woolworth opened his first store an established retailer across the street immediately responded to Woolworth's grand opening by hanging a sign on his store, "Doing business in the same spot for over fifty years." The next day Woolworth responded with a sign on his new store, "Established a week ago, no old stock." What a great example of repositioning a competitor's strength into a weakness.

If you want to take market share from your competition, learn how to reposition their strength into a weakness. It may take some work but it will be worth it.

....

Become a Doctor of Selling

Psychologists tell us that while there are three major buying motives (pain, fear, pleasure) by far the most common reason people buy is to eliminate psychological pain. Something is wrong in their personal or business lives that they want fixed and they are prepared to pay to fix it.

The best sales professionals never really sell anything. They offer solutions to their prospect's problems.

The uncover pain and make it go away. Why? Because the best sales-people understand that while people make decisions *intellectually* they buy *emotionally*.

Once you accept the fact that people buy emotionally, you will quickly realize that selling features and benefits does not work. Feature and benefit selling elicits a "think it over" or price comparison response, whereas finding pain will get you the order.

How do we find this elusive pain? We do it by telling stories and asking questions. Usually it takes three or more questions to get to pain. Prospects will not tell you the real reason up front; they will usually give you an intellectual smoke screen. People buy for their reasons, not yours, and until you uncover those reasons or pain, your chance of doing business is slim.

The dictionary defines pain as suffering or hurt, but in sales pain is something that makes your prospect uncomfortable, is personal, and gives you leverage in the selling process. The salesperson's job is to find someone who has pain, is committed to eliminating the pain, is willing to pay to get rid of it, and is in a position to make the decision. You cannot create pain, because that is manipulation. Instead, you help the prospect discover his or her pain by gently asking probing questions.

Pain will get you the sale; price will not. So become a Doctor of Sales and learn to uncover your customer's pain and the sales will follow!

....

The Art of Asking
Effective Questions

Suppose you are the CFO of a medium sized manufacturing firm and you have plans to meet with two agents from different insurance agencies.

The agent from agency A sits down and does a few things to establish rapport. Then he starts telling you about his company, its reputation, and commitment to quality service. Soon he goes into his presentation about their service standards, number of markets, and risk management philosophy, and asks you for an opportunity to provide a competitive quote to see how they compare.

The agent from agency B come in, and after doing a few things to establish rapport, she begins with a brief story to gain some credibility, and then asks a few questions.

Producer:

"Recently during a meeting with the executive of a manufacturing firm, the CFO told me his greatest concern was that all of the services available to him were poorly coordinated and because of that he didn't feel he was getting all that he was paying for. What he said he wanted was a more defined annual service plan that was proactive in nature, and would help him exercise maximum control to prevent and manage losses. We gave him

that and, as a result, his cost of losses has decreased by over 37%. I don't suppose that you are concerned with anything like that are you?"

Prospect:

"That's been a significant challenge. I don't have the time to really manage all the aspects to make sure they happen."

Producer:

"Just out of curiosity, when your agent came out at renewal to go through your service plan and laid out when he would deliver policies, review claims, review your mod worksheet, review payroll, and set up a renewal strategy so you wouldn't waste your time or overpay for your insurance, were you comfortable with how they laid everything out?"

Prospect:

"It's never been that formal a process."

Producer:

"Well, maybe it's not that important because you've never had an unpaid claim or an extensive audit."

Prospect:

"Wait a minute – this is important. If we had been doing this last year we wouldn't have had the surprise with..."

Which of these approaches best describes your selling style?

Remember that people like to buy but they don't like to be sold. The only way they can do that is by selling you why they want to buy. Instead of trying to persuade, convince or pitch someone why they should buy your product or service learn *The Art of Asking Effective Questions* and let them sell you. You'll make more sales and have a lot more fun doing so.

....

Everything Is Considered A Commodity

The emerging market forces of technology, competition, globalization, regulation and consolidation ensure that few products are truly unique for very long. These same forces have become the *Driving Forces of Commoditization*.

Everything is more complex.

Gone are the days *when* a company would develop a new product or process that could be easily understood by customers and clients. Technology alone has introduced more complexity into everything. Instead of making life simpler, it has had the opposite effect of complicating our lives.

So what's this got to do with selling?

Fast-forward a few frames in your prospects mind. Prospects don't fully comprehend the complexity of the problems they experience or the solutions that are available. Because the human mind tends to compress complex data into easily understood thoughts and ideas, your prospect resorts to making complex buying decisions based on things they can easily understand. And because they are overwhelmed with complexity, their mind tends to simplify the decision process by lumping all competitive products as basically the same, in other words, a commodity.

If the prospect mistakenly thinks there is no difference in a competitor's products, and that they are all pretty much the same, what criteria do they use to make their decision?

You got it. PRICE.

Think about it. If you think "term insurance is term insurance" or "bank loans are bank loans" or "computers are computers" then the only logical reason to choose one over the other is price.

How as a professional sales person can you get the prospect to understand that what you sell is different and not a commodity?

You need a redirect strategy that takes the conversation away from the product itself.

How to Avoid The Commodity Trap

How as a professional salesperson can you get the prospect to understand that what you sell is different and not a commodity? The answer to this question has more with how you do it rather than what you do.

Selling is about style.

Style is not an intellectual thing. It is an emotional feeling you get when you are in the presence of someone who has it. All things being equal, namely price and product, the salesperson with the most style and ability to connect at an emotional level with the prospect will get the business most of the time.

If this is true then how do you display your style? One of the ways is to behave in a manner that is exactly opposite of your competition. Instead of pitching, convincing and quoting try becoming a consultant by asking questions, listening and probing to help the prospect discover for themselves what their problems are and ignore the temptation to volunteer information and educate the prospect with your vast array of product knowledge.

In doing this the prospect will come to understand that you are different and do not fit the stereotype of a salesperson. When you do this your prospect will sense that you are different and will open up and begin to share information with you that will help you position yourself as a Trusted Advisor.

....

What To Do When The Prospect Just Wants You To Bid

Often times prospects put out a Request For Proposal, and expect a response from all the "vendors" they send it to. When you receive one of these RFPs what should you do? Good question. Before we answer it, let's take a look at what is happening.

What most likely is happening is that your prospect is entertaining bids or proposals from several of your competitors, or they may have even decided on a vendor already, and are looking for your proposal to keep your competitor honest.

When you comply with the RFP you are accepting their agenda and are playing by their rules. If you play by their rules, and respond to their process you are doing exactly what every one of your competitors is doing. There is no differentiation between you and your competitors except price. And if you are not low price, you don't usually get the business.

There is another problem in doing this. By responding, you are assuming that the prospect understands fully the problems, issues and concerns that they are hoping your product or service will eliminate. That assumption, which leads to a premature presentation, is wrong most of the time.

Instead, you should respond by sending a letter or making a phone call politely explaining why you don't answer RFPs or bids and why it isn't appropriate for either party to do business this way. The letter should make it very clear that you would like to talk with them to explore the full range of their issues to determine if you may be of service to them. If they choose not to do this then that is their choice.

At some point you must eventually get face to face with them if they are to become a client. Why not start that process early? Do this and you will eliminate a lot of wasted time.

Why You Should Not Listen To Most So Called Marketing Experts

There are an endless number of marketing experts and business people who will line up to tell you how direct response marketing doesn't work. Don't you fall for that line of faulty thinking because direct response marketing is alive and well.

A Real Example

As a direct response experiment, I recently wrote a 10 page sales letter and order form and used it at one of my day long seminars. With 10 pages to read, I correctly assumed that the participants would need some time to peruse it before I made the offer, so I put the letter only on the table in front of them before the seminar started.

After the last afternoon break, I passed out the order form and took 5 minutes explaining the offer and how to fill out the order form. I was very direct that this offer was only good the day of the seminar. (Actually, it was only good until I left the building.)

The Results

The full color sales letter and order form were printed on high quality semi gloss paper, and cost about $4.00 each to have designed and printed. At the seminar, I distributed 30 letters. When I finished my seminar, 8 of the 30 sales people ordered a specially designed package of sales tools and products. One additional company owner enrolled in our year long Masters Sales Program. The total revenue from these 9 new customers was $5300.00.

The total return on my $120.00 (30 letters x $4.00 @)) direct response investment was 4,416 percent! That's $177.00 for each of the 30 people in the audience whether they bought anything or not. At that rate, I only have to speak to 5,650 people to sell ONE MILLION dollars worth of products and tools. The only question is how fast I am going to do this.

....

Why Do Businesses Lose Customers

The reasons may surprise you. According to well documented studies businesses lose customers for the following reasons:

1%   die

3%   move away

5%   leave and do business with another company because for a recommendation from a friend of relative

9%   leave and do business with another company because they perceive that the other company has better products, services or prices

14% leave because they are dissatisfied with the product or the service

Add all of those together and you only have 32%. That leaves 68% of the customers who defect to your competitors unaccounted for. What other reasons could there possibly be for why customers defect? It is not what you think.

Buckle your seat belt because the answer will knock your socks off. Here it is.

Sixty-Eight (68) percent of customers who leave one company and start doing business with another company do so because they feel that their business was taken for granted...

...by a company who displayed an attitude of indifference.

That's right they don't feel appreciated, valued or cared for. It is the same reason why many employees leave jobs and why many wives leave husbands. William James, the father of modern psychology, said that the greatest human emotional need is the need to be recognized and appreciated.

In Abraham Maslow's hierarchy of needs the need to be loved and cared for is the third most basic human need behind the physiological need for food and water and the need for shelter and safety.

In our fast paced dehumanized world employees and customers are starved for a little personal attention that validates their existence.

What are you doing to let your employees and customers know that you value and appreciate them? Do you have a customer and employee appreciation practice at your company? Do you really care?

....

Your Limbic Brain Conspires to Keep You from Making Good Decisions

According to accepted neuroscience, we have three brains: our brain stem, which controls motor function, our limbic or emotional brain and our neo cortex or rational thinking brain.

Our limbic, emotional brain, which is some 400 million years older than our neo cortex is primitive. Its purpose is to ensure survival, and all the complicated emotions and behaviors that survival implies. It is here that our basest of instincts thrive: sex, fury, fight. It is short term oriented, visual, concrete and self centered, and it is not designed to deal with abstract, complex concepts and ideas.

Ruled by the limbic brain, our ancestors were obsessed with consuming vital resources to keep them alive. They were consumption oriented not savings oriented. They were short term, immediate gratification oriented. They never thought about storing and saving because they never knew if they were going to survive from one day to the next. Consequently, they consumed not saved.

According to Robert Trivers, an evolutionary biologist at Rutgers University, "There isn't necessarily a stop mechanism in us that says, 'Relax, you've got enough.' We've evolved to be maximizing machines."

For our ancestors the best way to save for the future was to consume now. Eating as much as they could, whenever they could, they were able to store extra calories in their bodies, in the hopes that this would carry them through any lean times that lay ahead.

This ancestrally dominated mindset has created many modern day problems: the tendency to spend and consume without any regard to the long term consequences, the addiction to instant gratification and the rejection of self denial and sacrifice, lack of patience and civility in society, micro term decision making by business and political leaders and on and on and on.

According to some Evolutionary Psychologists, our thinking, analytical, neo cortex brain has not evolved to keep pace with our complex, break neck speed society. Consequently, we are trying to cope in a complicated, frenetic world by using a brain that was designed to deal with much more basic human needs.

If our rational, analytical, thinking neo-cortex were truly in charge of our behavior we would engage in rational, intelligent, and civilized ways, but one does not have to look far to see the consequences of a society void of rational thought and dominated by the short term, emotionally motivated limbic brain.

Next time you make a decision, any decision, ask yourself *is this a thoroughly planned, rationally thought out decision or am I making a decision based on short term, emotional gratification?* If you are truly self aware and honest your answer will astound you.

....

How Emotionally Intelligent Are You

Recent research and field data support the premise that Emotional Intelligence is a major contributing factor to sales success. Daniel Goleman and Cary Cherniss in their book *The Emotionally Intelligent Workplace* evaluated three predictors of job success; Relevant Experience, Emotional Intelligence, and Outstanding IQ. They found that job success could be predicted:

> 71% of the time by the candidate's Relevant Experience

> 74% of the time by the candidate's Emotional Intelligence

> 48% of the time by the candidate's IQ

Goleman and Cherniss go on to say that the higher and more significant the position, the greater the role Emotional Intelligence plays. In fact, at the Top Sales and Senior Executive level, EI factors are as much as 80% responsible for long-term success.

According to Stephen Blakesley, President of Management Systems, Inc., numerous studies specific to sales and Emotional Intelligence found:

In one organization, sales reps with high EI were 127 times more productive than sales reps that had average EI.

In another large, multinational organization sales people selected on the basis of Emotional Intelligence sold, on average $91,370 more annually than other sales people in the organization.

Additionally, those selected on the basis of Emotional Intelligence had 63% less turnover during the first year than those selected based on experience.

No doubt about it. Emotional Intelligence is more important than experience when it comes to success in sales.

....

Establishing Agendas

When you first meet with a buyer /prospect, it is important that both of you are on the same page about what will happen during the meeting. In order to have an effective meeting, both you and the buyer/prospect must agree to what will happen, when it will happen and in what order it will happen. To this end it is important that you use an agenda to eliminate any potential misunderstandings.

Creating agendas with buyers happen at the beginning and end of each contact or conversation. Failure to do this results in the sales person making a lot of assumptions, most of which will be false.

Below is a meeting agenda that we teach our clients to use in their first face to face meeting. We suggest that you spend two minutes going over this agenda and gaining agreement with your buyer before you begin any substantive discussions. If you will use this you will shorten your sales cycle and avoid a lot of misunderstandings.

Meeting Agenda

1. Meeting Objective: Is there a fit between your company and ours?

2. Two Ground Rules:

   Total Honesty and Openness with each other.

   It is OK for either of us to terminate the conversation at any time.

3. Your Issues:

   Current Situation < ------ > Desired Situation

4. Overview of our company's products and services

   What we do, how we do it, how much does it cost?

5. Decision Process

   How do you make decisions and what do you need from me to help you do that?

6. Next Step:

   Clearly decide what our next step should be

Understanding Prospects Buying Styles

The Key to Developing Trust and Credibility

Buyers have many different likes, dislikes and motivations. Top performing sales professionals know that the key to developing trust and credibility is to expertly determine the likes, dislikes and buying styles of their prospects and to adapt their communication style to match that of their buyer.

Some buyers:

- Like to have fun.

- Like new products.

- Like proven products.

- Like a lot of data.

- Like you to be direct.

- Like personal talk.

- Like time to think.

- Like to negotiate.

- Like showy products.

- Like traditional products **and**

- **Some don't...**

The key to building trust and credibility is determining the buying style of the prospect or buyer. Expert sales communicators understand this, are able to recognize the buying style of their buyer, and adapt their communication style to match the buyer.

Buying styles are nothing new. Hippocrates first observed this around 460 BC when he first categorized the four styles of human behavior. Even though the terms have changed over the years social psychologists still agree that there are four distinct behavioral styles.

Let's take a look at the characteristics of the four basic styles, how to recognize them and how to effectively communicate with them:

The Driver

This extroverted buying style is a very bottom line cut to the chase type of buyer. They are direct, forceful, aggressive, decisive, competitive, results oriented, impatient and are quick decision makers.

They are primarily interested in the answer to the question *"What can you or your product or service do for me?"*

Examples of this style are Ross Perot, Hillary Clinton, Barbara Walters and Fidel Castro.

When communicating with these buyers be clear, specific and to the point. Don't ramble or waste their time. They are interested in new and innovative products and services. When talking with these folks stick to business and avoid any effort to socialize or chit chat.

The Social

This buying style is a super extrovert. They are very talkative, socially engaging, enthusiastic, charming, gregarious, optimistic, inspiring, and tend to be impulsive decision makers.

They are primarily interested in the answer to the question *"Why should I do business with you or your company instead of someone else?"*

Examples of this style are Arnold Schwarzenegger, Oprah Winfrey, Andre Agassi, Dolly Parton.

When communicating with these folks allow time for some socialization and don't be cold or curt. Ask them questions that allow them to talk about their goals. Don't dwell on facts and figures. Provide testimonials from people they view as important or prominent.

They are interested in new, showy, and innovative products and services.

The Amiable

This buying style is introverted and reserved. They are relaxed, serene, non-demonstrative and are shy and hesitant to open up or share any information about themselves or their situation.

Because they are hesitant and slow to develop trust they want to know *"Who else in my industry are you working with?"*

Examples of this style are children's television host Mr. Rogers, Mother Teresa, Magic Johnson and Tom Brokaw.

When communicating with these buying styles patiently listen and be responsive. Provide plenty of proof and statistics. Take it slow and easy and don't force a quick decision.

They are slow decision makers who like traditional, proven products, guarantees and assurances.

The Analytical

This introverted buying style is methodical, very skeptical, cautious, evasive, analytical, systematic and precise. They will ask a lot of questions and not want to reveal much of anything.

They are perfectionists who want to know *"How does this exactly work?"* and *"Why is it done that way?"* and *"What data do you have to support your claims"?*

Examples of this style are Diane Sawyer, Jack Nicklaus, Ted Koppel. Because of the exacting nature they tend to be in such professions as accounting, architecture, banking, engineering and law.

When communicating with these buying styles approach them in a direct, straightforward way and be very specific and have data to support everything you say. Use a logical approach. Present specifics and details. Provide them with the information and the time they need to make a decision.

They need a lot of proof and background information before they will make a purchasing decision an they need plenty of time to absorb and digest facts before making a decision.

They are highly suspicious of new and unproven products. When presenting to them use plenty of research information and testimonials.

Questions for You to Consider

- What is your natural selling style?

- Which buying style is the most difficult for you to connect with?

- Which style do you tend to avoid?

- What do you need to do to become a more skilled communicator?

....

Sales Jobs Still Seen With Contempt

A recent study conducted by Development Dimensions International, a human resources company, found that 41 percent of consumers surveyed rated the sales profession below mediocre. And one in five consumers surveyed said they believe salespeople's expertise is getting worse.

Not only do consumers see salespeople as incompetent they see sales as an undesireable profession. Survey results reported that 46 percent of those surveyed say they would be ashamed to call themselves a salesperson. (I wonder how many salespeople feel the same way)

The good news in all of this is that buyers still rank salespeople as their number two source of product information. Second to only the internet but ahead of family and friends. Says Bradford Thomas, the company's sales practice team manager, "In a given week, people make dozens or hundreds of purchase decisions but see the process as a necessary evil. It's something people have to do but they are not always that jazzed about it. They're dealing with salespeople way more that they want to."

How about you? Are you perceived in your maketplace as a welcomed guest or an unwanted pest?

Look Who Is Using Direct Response Marketing To Boost Sales

In the Sunday, April 6th, 2008 issue of The Tennessean, the Nashville daily newspaper, David Bohan, founder of Bohan Advertising and Marketing writes about the resurgence of direct response marketing.

In his article Bohan, points out that contrary to popular belief people actually look forward to reading their mail daily. According to the U S Postal Service consumers spend 30 minutes a day reading their mail.

Smart direct marketers are taking advantage of this by selectively targeting niches and crafting messages that have high appeal to their audience. This market segmentation and quality copy is producing incredible results for those marketers who have honed their direct marking skills.

"The offer is the hero of the direct mail piece, but the creative is the sizzle", says Chris Kelman, creative director of Catapult Marketing in Westport, Connecticut.

Using market segmentation, Kimberly Clark's Huggies brand created a direct response program that targeted mothers by the age of their babies from pre-natal through a child's 30th month. The long copy, information rich content focused on benefits of Huggies and directed mothers to the Huggies web site where they could obtain additional information.

Instead of trying to sell the mothers directly, the direct response campaign "sold" the mothers on going to the web site where they were offered more information, coupons to use and contests to enter. Every click of the mouse brought the mothers deeper and deeper into the sales funnel where they were giving their permission to be sold and marketed to.

Using Direct Response to Sell Season Football Tickets

One of the most prestigious football programs in the country is the University of Alabama. In Alabama football is more than a game. It borders on being a religion. That being the case you would think that selling season tickets would not require a direct mail campaign. If you think that you would be wrong.

Seems as though the Crimson Tide has found a marketing strategy that will be copied as fast as you can say "Roll Tide Roll".

In 2007, the University of Alabama's Athletic Department hit the jackpot by developing a personalized ad campaign that was directed to season ticket holders. This campaign featured a postcard of Bryant Denny Stadium with the recipient's name spelled out on the field by the Alabama Band. The postcard also included a personalized URL that directed ticket holders to a web site where the Alabama cheerleaders held up signs with their name on them.

The result: online renewals doubled from the previous year.

Smart marketers are reexamining their thoughts of direct response marketing when designing marketing campaigns. Maybe it is time you consider doing the same.

Are You Going To Be Relevant In The Future

In a study done at Columbia University, it was determined that the top 20% of sales reps earn 16 times more income than bottom 80%, and the top 4% of sales reps earn 54 times more income than the bottom 80%.

Additional data confirms that 65% of everything that is sold in North America is sold by 15% of the sales people.

These numbers should be a wakeup call for owners, managers and sales reps.

Why Should You Care About Any of This?

That is a fair but naïve question to ask. If you are a manager you should realize that about one - third of your sales force is actually a profit center. The other two – thirds, while somewhat productive, are barely covering their cost.

If, as predicted by some, employee cost will more than double in the next forty-eight months this should scare the living hell out of YOU.

When this happens, I predict that companies will have a significant reduction in force of their sales teams, and that only the sales people who are determined to be a profit center will be retained. If you are a mediocre or marginal producer this should scare the hell out of YOU.

The End of the Company Gravy Train Is Insight

For too long companies and managers have tolerated mediocrity and provided what amounts to corporate welfare to non productive sales people.

Because of shrinking margins, increased competition, and the need to increase productivity, companies can no longer do this and remain competitive and profitable. In the future, every employee from receptionist to CEO will have to prove their profitability. If they can't they will be sacked and rightly so.

Many employees somehow think that it is their birth right to be provided with a good paying job which doesn't require a great deal from them other than showing up and putting in their time. They have forgotten or never learned that in a Capitalistic Society rewards only come to those who provide value in the market place. No value no pay. Not a hard lesson to learn but one that the liberal do gooders of this world avoid talking about. Instead they pander to the lazy masses that willingly lap up their message, "that the government will take care of you", like a cat laps up warm milk.

What Can You Do to Prepare For This

Accept one – hundred percent responsibility for your own future. It is not your company's, or the country's responsibility to provide you with the skills and talents you need to excel.

Invest YOUR time and money in competent training and education that will make you more competitive and more skilled than your competitors both within and outside of your company.

Become a voracious reader, attend seminars and events and associate with the top performers in your industry, turn your vehicle into a rolling university and listen to audio training materials, stop hanging around time and energy vampires that suck life from you, and seek expert coaching. If you will do these things consistently you will be well positioned to weather the coming storm.

....

Who Is In Control

In the last 90 days have you given have you given a demo, a full blown quote or proposal or a presentation to a prospect, and then had them tell you they do not have any money or the project has been put on the back burner or they need to "think it over"?

If so, congratulations, you have just been "rolled."

Yes, you have been rolled, screwed, taken advantage of, out maneuvered, caught off guard and just plain beaten by a better sales person, and the sad fact is that you don't even have a clue it is happening.

It is incredible how naïve and ignorant most sales people are.

They blindly go through the motions of gathering information and making presentations and proposals without a hint of what will happen once they do so. They have been taught by equally ignorant sales managers that the key to success is giving a lot of presentations and proposals, and if they will do so things will work out fine. They blindly and relentlessly do this even though it only results in a sale 20% – 30% of the time.

This is incredibly stupid when you consider that, at best, 70% of their time and effort is wasted giving proposals to prospects who never buy.

Recently, I was talking with my neighbor, a sales person, who works for a local contractor. He was lamenting to me how many bids his company was doing but how few jobs they were actually getting. When I asked him what percentage of bids that he submitted resulted in contracts he said, "No more than 10%"? I then said to him, "you mean 90% of the bids you submit you end up not getting paid for"? His response was, "you know I never thought of it that way because that's the way it's done in the construction industry. If you don't bid you don't get the job."

Trying to let him off easy because he is a good neighbor, I then asked him how much did it cost his company to produce a bid, he responded, "I dunno, maybe thousands".

Thousands!! What a terrible business model. How can a company make money when 90% of their new business acquisition activity results in failure?

Think about that for a moment. They are not being paid for ninety percent of the man hours that they devote to estimating, drawing of prints, meetings with contractors, in-house staff meetings, sales presentations, etc. That sucks like a Hoover.

I then probed deeper, "how much does it cost your company to acquire a new customer", "I dunno", he said. Now mind you this is not some rookie sales person. This person has been in sales for over 30 years.

Although it is a stretch, he might be forgiven for not knowing this information, but his boss, the owner of the company, cannot be forgiven for not knowing this information.

How about you **do you know how much of your time is wasted** and how much you don't get paid for? **Do you know how much it cost to acquire a new customer for you business?** If you do email me sclark@ newschoolselling.com and let me know.

Life Is A Lot Better Than Many Would Have You Believe

The latest form of political incorrectness is positive thinking. Politicians and the media both would have you believe that the economy is going to hell in a hand basket. That kind of thinking is utter rubbish when you analyze and study the economic data.

The mental attitude of a large portion of the population thinks things are awful, terrible, horrible or worse. The data would indicate that they are wrong.

The Data

Unemployment is at 5.5%, low by historical standards; income is rising slightly ahead of inflation; housing prices are down but the typical house is still worth 30% more than it was worth in 2000; 94% of Americans are paying their mortgages on time and most of the other 6% will find ways to keep their homes.

Inflation was up in 2007, but for the last 16 years it has been low or almost non existent. Living standards for all economic classes, including the middle class and the low income group, is at an all time high.

All forms of pollution, other than greenhouse gases are in decline; cancer, heart disease, stroke incidence are declining; crime is in decline and education levels are at an all time high.

Sure gas prices are up, the dollar is weak and credit is tight but these are minor issues in an otherwise healthy economy.

In the late 70's and early 80's there was double digit interest rates, unemployment and runaway inflation. Personal income, as adjusted for inflation is up 20% since the 1960s. While there are still racial issues they are nothing like they were in the 1950's. When you compare those issues to the issues of today there is no comparison.

Why All the Pessimism

In order to understand what is going on you have to take a really hard look at who the purveyors of negativity are and then drill down to understand their agenda. Without a doubt the purveyors of negativity are the media - both electronic and print. The volume of their message and the size of their audience make it easy for them to influence, persuade and downright "brainwash" the uneducated, intellectually lazy, mass of humanity.

When one drills down on the stories that appear on the nightly news and the front pages of morning newspapers there is an unmistakable trend and it is all negative. Why the negative you might ask.

Good question.

The simple answer is that negative news sells newspapers and network airtime. And newspapers and networks make their money from advertising. The more viewers or readers the more the cost of the advertising space. The media knows all too well that the best way to drawn a crowd is to promote negative by showing natural disasters of epic proportion, gruesome murders, rapes, kidnappings, celebrity misfortunes, etc.

Politicians of all stripes know, just as well, that when people are stirred up and fearful they are more easily controlled. They then capitalize on this fear by promoting themselves as some sort of hero with a magic solution to a multitude of societal ills. It is in their best interest to do so. It is not in their best interest - unless they are in power- to promote optimism. All of this is very carefully controlled and orchestrated. If you think otherwise you are indeed naïve.

....

The Difference Between
Winners and Losers

According to one credible study done by a very large insurance company, the top 20% of life insurance agents make 16 times as much commissions as the bottom 80% and the top 4% of agents make 54 times as much as the bottom 80%. If you are not in the life insurance business don't make the mistake of thinking that this only applies to life insurance and that somehow your business is different or unique. It is not.

If you spent 25 years chronicling the behavioral differences between the mediocre majority and high achieving minority as I have, the most striking distinction you would find is this:

Winners stick to things and don't give up or quit, losers give up easily and flit about randomly.

Losers look for the next new shiny object, modern fantasy or magic elixir. Winners find winning strategies and stick to applying them.

Winners stay stuck like super glue to an objective, purpose and goal; acquiring the needed knowledge; ignoring criticism; refusing to take no for a permanent answer, fighting, scrapping studying, figuring out one more piece of the success puzzle and then another and another; these behaviors are behind the true stories of the rich and famous.

Sadly, the mediocre majority don't stick too much of anything. They have little discipline and patience to stick to the behaviors that produce success. Their life's report card is filled with "Incompletes"; books purchased but not read, audio programs purchased but not listened to, good intentions begun but not completed, projects started but never finished. Their desks and homes are littered with worthwhile projects and files still-born in procrastination and strangled in disorganization. Losers display poor discipline, are intellectually uncurious, are uninformed, have self limiting beliefs, display poor physical conditioning, and have sloppy nutritional habits.

The reasons people don't stick to anything long enough to succeed are many and varied. Some are psychological, revealed in a book I recommend. *The New Psycho-Cybernetics* by Dr. Maxwell Maltz and Dan Kennedy. It and the previous edition have sold over 30 million copies worldwide. Some are circumstantial; people who permit themselves and their time to be ruled by others' priorities. Some are sinful like sloth. For many it is the desire for success without the personal responsibility that must accompany success. Whatever the losers lack of "stick-to-itiveness", the winners refuse to be deterred or distracted from their objectives and the relentless pursuit of them.

The bottom line is that the successful achievement of exceptional goals requires two key elements: acquisition of new knowledge and information by sticking to a course of regimented study and learning even if it is uncomfortable, foreign or difficult; being disciplined to stick to self imposed requirements to implement what is learned no matter how difficult or uncomfortable.

....

Can Your Brain Be Tricked By Price?

Does the price you paid for that expensive wine at dinner influence your satisfaction with that wine? The answer to this question may reside in the folds of your medial orbitofrontal cortex, the part of the brain that registers pleasure.

In what should be music to the ears of marketers, the old adage that you get what you pay for really is true when it comes to that most ephemeral of products: bottled wine.

The Research

A recent study by Baba Shiv, an Associate Professor of Marketing at Stanford University's Graduate School of Business, and a group of researchers at California Institute of Technology concludes that people will experience an increase in activity and pleasure within the brain when they consume wine that they perceive to be expensive even though the part of the brain that interprets taste is not affected.

While many studies have looked at how marketing affects behavior, this is the first to show that it has a direct effect on the brain.

In an article, co-authored by Baba Shiv, titled "Marketing Actions Can Modulate Neural Representations of Experienced Pleasantness," published online Jan. 14 in the *Proceedings of the National Academy of Sciences*, students were placed in a MRI and given sips of red wine-including the same one twice, with different price tags: $5.00 (the actual price) and $45.00 (a fictional price).

The subjects reported that they liked the expensive wine more than the cheaper wine even though it was the same wine - a preference that was mirrored by an increased activity in the medial orbitofrontal cortex of their brains as measured by Magnetic Resonance Imaging.

The Marketing Implications

According to Shiv, the traditional assumption in economics is that a person's "experienced pleasantness" (EP) from consuming a product depends only on its intrinsic properties and the individual's thirst. Contrary to this basic assumption, several studies have shown that marketing can influence how people value goods. For example, Shiv has shown that people who paid a higher price for an energy drink, such as Red Bull, were able to solve more brain teasers than those who paid a discounted price for the same product.

Despite the pervasive influence of marketing, very little is known about how neural mechanisms affect decision-making, the researchers said.

"Here, we propose a mechanism though which marketing actions can affect decision-making," they write. "We hypothesized that changes in the price of a product can influence neural computations associated with EP." Because perceptions about quality are positively correlated with price, the scholars argued that someone might expect an expensive wine to taste better than a cheaper one.

Says Baba Shiv, "What we document is that price is not just about inferences of quality, but it can actually affect real quality. So, in essence, [price] is changing people's experiences with a product and, therefore, the outcomes from consuming this product."

The lesson says Baba Shiva is that: "there's a temptation among marketers to keep reducing prices. We're saying be careful before you embark on that strategy."

In keeping with this research marketers would do well to position themselves as the most expensive product or service in their market category. Doing so could actually become smart positioning.

I realize this positioning is counterintuitive to the prevailing thought that most marketers have, and that many readers will have difficulty with this concept.

My study of marketing has demonstrated that most marketers want to position themselves somewhere in the middle of the price range in their marketplace. This positioning eliminates any competitive advantage by creating a "me too" perception in the marketplace.

A Personal Experience

Several years ago, I experimented with this concept by running a year long radio campaign that stated in every ad that "our training is expensive and difficult". Instead of turning buyers away it actually attracted more of my ideal clients. Interestingly, when prospects became clients their training experience was enhanced because they paid a handsome sum to participate, and they would often brag to others about how "expensive and difficult" their training was.

Sure I lost some potential clients, but I repelled a far greater number of wimps, weasels and yahoos that I had no interest in working with. The clients I attracted were among the elite in their sales profession. They were committed sponges who soaked up every thing they could and they were a pleasure to work with. Since then, I have raised my prices several times, and every time I do so I get more clients and better quality clients.

As a side note, two years after the radio campaign finished I spoke at a local Rotary Club. Before my presentation, I gave the president, who was to introduce me, a written introduction for him to read. When he got up to introduce me he said, "well I had an introduction to read to you about our guest but I can't find it. All I can remember about him is that his name is Steve Clark and you have probably heard his radio ads that talk about how expensive he is. So give a big Rotary welcome to Steve Clark." That is the power of positioning.

A Military Application

Positioning is not lost on the United States Marine Corps. They are well aware of this concept and position themselves as the elite branch of military service. Their campaign for "a few good men" and "we don't accept applications only commitments" is a practical application of positioning to attract the best. And while other branches of service struggle to meet their recruiting goals the Marine Corps does just fine.

How about you? Have you intentionally positioned your company as the elite in your industry or have you unintentionally positioned your company as just a little bit above average? If you have unintentionally positioned yourself anywhere in the middle of the pack, remember that only the lead dog ever gets a change of scenery.

....

Ten Creative Ways to Raise Your Prices and Fees

The idea of raising prices or increases fees strikes fear into the heart of most marketers, sales people and business owners. Most of these folks have the mistaken notion that if they raise prices they will have a mass exodus of existing clients and will repel future clients.

This visceral fear is not substantiated by data. In marketing study after study, price is never the number one issue that buyers use to determine who they are going to do business with. In fact, these studies show that less than 10% of buyers use price as their primary criteria for making a buying decision.

Below are ten strategies that you can use when you get your head straight about positioning your price. While you may not be able to implement all of these ten strategies, read each of them carefully and ponder how you might creatively use them in your business.

1. Raise your current prices and fees

This is a no brainer and requires little skill. However, it does require a lot of courage. The reality is that people will pay you more than you are currently asking. Maybe not 50% or 100% more but certainly 10% - 30% or more. All you have to do is convince yourself of this and transfer this conviction and confidence to your buyers.

2. Change your target market

Start going after the type of clients who are not price shoppers. While price is a consideration in most buying decisions, research shows that less than 10% of buyers buy strictly on price. You must retrain yourself that price is not the reason most people don't buy from you. It may be that they don't need what you sell, they don't trust you, they don't see you as an expert or they don't see the value in what you offer. Whatever the reason that they don't buy, it isn't price.

3. Stop giving stuff away for free

Sales people are notorious for giving away products and services for free. Some where in their head they have the idea that if they will be nice and give "more value" (that usually means the company's resources) they will be elevated and achieve exalted status in the eyes of the buyer. That's rubbish. The reality is that the more you give away the more they want for free and the harder it becomes to get them to pay for future products or services. The solution: Charge for everything.

4. Bundle products and services together

Instead of selling individual items, start selling packages by bundling various products and services together into one sale. It is much easier to sell three items as a package deal than it is to make three individual sales.

5. Sell a deluxe version of your product and service

Offer a premium or deluxe version of what you sell. At least 20% of your buyers will upgrade and buy the "platinum" version of your product or service. This is easy money that you are leaving on the table. The more affluent the buyer the more likely they are to want the "upscale" version.

6. Up sell with the current sale

Once you make a sale give the buyer an irresistible offer to buy an additional product or service or add on as part of the original order. Present this as a one time offer and have the guts to stick to it. You will be amazed at how many people will buy it because they don't want to let the opportunity pass them by.

7. Up sell immediately after the sale

Immediately after the sale offer the buyer an opportunity to purchase an additional product or service within a very limited time frame. This offer can be made via the phone or mail or in person.

8. Build in a renewal program

Offer an automatic renewal program that will lock your customers into future purchases unless they opt out of the program. This eliminates the need to sell them every time your current contract expires.

9. Change what you sell and how you sell it

Develop and offer a continuity program so that you get ongoing, residual, monthly income from each account or customer. Radio examples of this might include offering a marketing newsletter paid subscription to clients and prospects, monthly advertising teleclass sessions or live marketing and advertising workshops, etc. Sell once and get paid repeatedly. These could also be bundled together with an ad campaign or they could be stand alone sales that could be leveraged into future advertising sales.

10. Get creative about developing new non traditional revenue sources.

There are many low cost creative ways to generate additional revenue. Take off your myopic glasses and get outside of your industry by studying and analyzing what other businesses are doing that you can reengineer to work in your business.

Creativity, no matter what industry, rarely comes from within that industry. If you want to stand out, stop thinking that somehow your business is different and that what works in one industry will not work in your industry. The reality is that if something works in one industry it can, in most cases with some creativity, work in your business.

Most Managers Don't Have a Clue

As I continue to coach and consult with entrepreneurs, owners and managers of sales organizations, I continue to be amazed at how little they know about how their sales people spend their time. When I ask managers the question, "where do your people spend their time", the response most often is, "I don't have a clue".

Accountability is the most difficult and second most important job of a sales manager. Only hiring and recruiting is more important. The gathering of real information about what is going on in the field should be at the top of every manager's daily activity.

Why is this so important

Truth be known most sales people are undisciplined, lazy, and notoriously poor planners and managers of their time. This has been confirmed by a study at Columbia University, in which, thousands of sales people were tracked, and it was determined that the average sales person was productive only two hours out of an eight hour work day. If this is true, then what in the world are they doing with the other 75% of their work day? And more importantly how much more productive could they be if they got organized and had a plan?

Why does this issue exist

It exists for several reasons: first, managers are oblivious to what is going on in the field because they spend most of their time shuffling papers, compiling reports and attending meetings instead of getting out in the field with their reps on a daily basis. Secondly, many managers intuitively know this is going on but they don't have the courage to confront the issue and deal with it. They would prefer to ignore it and hope it goes away.

Third, most managers are poorly trained and ill equipped to skillfully handle this and a myriad of other important sales management functions. Fourth, mangers themselves are no better at personal discipline, planning, organization and time management than the people they are trying to lead.

What's the solution

The big picture solution is that...

...companies need a sales management operations manual that spells out the roles and responsibilities and gives each manager the tools to do their job.

Secondly, managers need intensive training on how to perform their job.

A simple solution for the time management issue is to have each sales rep keep a time log and account for their use of time. This log should be broken down in fifteen minute increments and sales reps should be required to turn this in to the manager at the end of each day or each week.

I realize that many managers will resent having to do this because they perceive this as baby sitting or micro management. If you have any of these feelings you need to get over it and realize that most of your people are incapable of self management at this point.

If you will implement this tough accountability and begin to train and teach your people how to become more disciplined, organized planners and managers of their time you will not have to do this forever. If you fail to take on this managerial responsibility you will continue to have poor or mediocre production from most of your sales staff.

Get Your **FREE** Audio CD: *Prospecting to Fill the Pipeline*

Printed in the USA
CPSIA information can be obtained
at www.ICGtesting.com
JSHW012024140824
68134JS00033B/2858